STARTING THERAPY

A GUIDE TO GETTING READY, FEELING INFORMED, AND GAINING THE MOST FROM YOUR SESSIONS

FAITH FREED

APOCRYPHILE
PRESS

Apocryphile Press
1700 Shattuck Ave #81
Berkeley, CA 94709
www.apocryphilepress.com

Copyright © 2019 Faith Freed
Printed in the United States of America
ISBN 978-1-949643-31-2 | paperback
ISBN 978-1-949643-32-9 | ePub

CONTENTS

ACKNOWLEDGMENTS

The first time I considered therapy, it was at the suggestion of my parents. Somewhere in my early twenties, I got a phone call from my Mom. She told me, "Your father and I are getting a divorce" (...mic drop...). The next thing I remember, after some blah blah blah explanation, was, "You can go to therapy if you want. We'll pay for it."

"...Wow. Jeeze," I thought, struggling to absorb the shock. "So there's a consolation prize? I'll take it."

It turns out, the offer of therapy—just getting it on my radar as a resource, as well as initial funding—was a meaningful gift. Thanks to my unexpected inner exploration, all kinds of light bulbs went on. Eventually that included the inclination to pursue psychotherapy as a career.

Just as surely as I can trace starting therapy back to my parents, I can trace the birth of this book, *Starting Therapy*, directly to John Mabry. If he hadn't declared that a guide for starting therapy needed to be written, this book wouldn't exist. As soon as I heard John's idea, I knew he was right. Therapy needs to be demystified so no one misses out on giving it a try and reaping the life-changing benefits. There was only one thing to say: "I'm in." Fortunately, John had already written his illuminating and essential book, *Starting Spiritual Direction*, which he generously offered as a tried and true template to adopt and adapt. A simple thanks to John is not adequate, given that this book—from prompting to publication—is all thanks to him. Yes, atop his growing tower of award-winning titles, John knows the ever-changing publishing industry as well as the craft. He's also been an enthusiastic, encouraging, and wise mentor and a steady source of inspiration since we first met. John, thank you for being a rock star role model and trusting me with your brainstorm.

My gratitude extends to those who kindly agreed to be manuscript readers. First and foremost, my oldest son, Max, edited the first draft and offered advice and encouragement, from start to finish. His brother, Ned, was also on hand to offer indispensable editorial feedback on the fly. Colleagues and friends were wonderfully helpful as well. Among them, Sherry Cassedy, Dr. Kevin Pinjuv and Alex Grossman provided a well-rounded trio of feedback for which I'm deeply grateful. My husband, Eric, also weighed in on the work with the critique of someone who refuses to waste time. These days, that's a necessary perspective to have.

Huge thanks goes to all those who provided me with their juicy stories from the therapy room to retell in disguise. This book is based in truth, and that's thanks to the giving and brave informants who believe that their disclosure will be the reader's gain. Finally, heartfelt gratitude goes out to those who start therapy, so we can improve the world together, one person at a time.

FOREWORD

BY JOHN R. MABRY

The world needs this book.

You can't say that about a lot of books, not really. The world may want another Harry Potter book, but the world does not need it. Critics may applaud another deep dive into the life of one of our founding fathers, but do we need it, really? No. This book, though. This book we need.

Over half of Americans see a therapist (or other mental health professional) each year, but no one tells us how to prepare for this. For each one of us, our very first therapy session is an alien thing. All we have to go on are stereotypes culled from years of consuming media. Some of that gives us good information...most of it does not. What we need is an "Introduction to Therapy" course, maybe "Therapy 101." This book is the closest we are going to get to that.

This book demystifies the therapy process. This book tells us what to expect, and what not to expect. It tells us how to be ready for therapy, how to use the time in that little room to our best advantage. It gives us valuable information about what therapists actually do, how they are trying to help us, and how to make the most of the experience.

In short, it takes away the fear.

You can just feel the stress melt away as you read it. I know I did. As I read section after section, I just kept thinking, "I wish someone had given me this book before I started therapy." I would have spared myself a lot of anxiety and stumbling around.

Fortunately, this book is here now. If you are starting therapy for the first time, why are you wasting your time on a Foreword? Skip straight to Chapter One and dive in. This is for you. If you're an old hand at it, keep reading. Also, I hope you will purchase copies for friends and loved ones before they have their first session. They will thank you for it, and you can sleep easy knowing you've done your good deed for the day. Heck, I think it might count for two days—because it's a big assist.

Of course, I'm not really an objective observer. A couple of years ago, I wrote a book called *Starting Spiritual Direction*. I intended that book to be helpful for people who had never done spiritual direction before. It was a hit, and people all over the world have written to express their thanks for it. So that got me thinking…there ought to be a similar book for therapy.

Now, on the surface of it, therapy and spiritual direction look very similar. A client and a professional meet for an hour and talk. Afterwards, they make an appointment for next time. Some form of payment is usually exchanged. But the subject of the discussion is different in spiritual direction than it is in therapy. Still, it seemed to me that a book that had helped so many people prepare for spiritual direction needed an analog for those just starting therapy.

I am a spiritual director, not a therapist, so I knew I could not write that book. (I have been in therapy for most of my adult life. Does that make me a bit of an expert? Maybe, but not enough to write this book!) So I reached out to Faith Freed, a skilled psychotherapist and a former student of mine at the Institute of Transpersonal Psychology.

Faith had already written a fabulous book on forging one's

own spirituality, called *IS*. I thought *IS* was brilliant, so I knew she could write. I also knew that her friendly and down-to-earth style and humor were a perfect fit for the project.

I sent Faith a copy of *Starting Spiritual Direction*, and we met on a Sunday afternoon near the UC Berkeley campus to nosh on french fries and discuss it. She totally got it, and a few months later, she emailed me the manuscript. This book. And it was just as great as I'd hoped it would be.

At first, we thought we'd be co-authors, following the structure of my book. But as I read Faith's first draft I realized that this book had nothing to do with me—this book was Faith's, and Faith's alone. And it was *terrific*.

This is a helpful book, a necessary book. Please buy it for someone you know who is facing their first therapy session. It will be the most loving and caring thing you can do for them. If your child is starting therapy soon, read it yourself, and talk about some of the sections with your child to help them get ready.

I believe the biggest obstacle to effective therapy is *fear*. We go in resistant to the process, suspicious of the therapist, and pretty sure we do not want to be there. None of this helps therapy help us. But this book removes that fear. It is the antidote to fear. This book makes therapy a welcoming process, helps us warm up to it and our role in it. It helps us succeed.

Thank you, Faith, for writing a book that will help people to succeed in therapy. You might be thinking that all you did was write this nifty book. But, in fact, you have done something that is going to change people's lives.

John R. Mabry, PhD
September 2, 2019
Oakland, CA

INTRODUCTION

Your first therapy session ought to be fascinating. After all, your sessions are all about a subject dear to your heart—you! And you're not the only one who'll be intrigued with your inner world and curious to know you a lot better. Your therapist will be, as well. This partnership is unlike any other, because both parties come together to focus on your healing, happiness and highest good. This book is written for you, the client, and not the therapist, so simple language is used throughout. You'll notice that the word "client," rather than "patient," is used. There is no assumption that a desire to seek therapy indicates mental illness. To the contrary, enlisting a therapist is often a sign of good self-care. In many cases, therapy is a wise measure taken to cultivate and/or maintain a sense of balance and clarity. A person seeking therapy is not presumed "sick," so "patient" can sound a little extreme, although the terms *patient* and *client* are both commonly used.

The terms are not so important. What matters is that you care to attend to your psychological well-being. Those who stay on top of their overall health—mind, body and spirit—are inclined to pay attention to their mental health. If you work out for fitness, get a massage to relax and meditate to stoke your spiritual side, you might also get therapy to ease your mind and lighten your load.

It's remarkable how many people come for psychotherapy with the foundational intention to know, accept, like, and one day, truly love themselves. Sure, symptoms often drive that first visit: sadness, worry, confusion, life situations and discontent. But sometimes people who feel generally good about themselves seek therapy just to embark upon a personal growth journey or assimilate a new stage of life. No matter what initially gets you through your therapist's door, you're almost certain to gain useful tools that will benefit you over the long haul. So, what's it like to embark on an investment that will reap lifelong results? Let's take a look.

A seasoned psychotherapist, Margaret Walden, opens her door to welcome Jay, a 33-year-old man seeking therapy to address some distress about a recent break-up and concerns about his future dating prospects. He enters eagerly, clutching papers in his hand. "Hi, I'm Margaret." She greets him with a warm smile. "Hi...hi. Jay," he smiles back, seemingly relieved to be in the right place with someone clearly receptive and kind. "Here's the consent form," Jay says as he stiffly hands her the papers. "Do I sit here?" He gestures to the couch. "Yes, that's perfect," Margaret says. "Please make yourself comfortable." The therapist takes her chair across the coffee table from him. A box of tissues sits in the center of the table within reach. Even though clients tend to laugh as often as they cry, it's a reminder that all thoughts and feelings are welcome. Margaret makes sure the form is understood and signed, which secures the specifics of their agreement, including risks and benefits, as well as client confidentiality. There's a moment of silence. He glances around the room, his gaze finally landing on her. "So how does this work? I mean…what happens now?" She first suggests that they take a deep breath together, to help him relax and get present. Then she invites him to talk a bit about what brings him in. "I appreciate what you shared when we spoke on the phone," she says sincerely. "Would you like to say more about what you hope to get out of our time together?" And so it begins.

Like many first-time clients, Jay seems slightly uncomfortable with the process, not knowing what to expect. This is natural and quite common. Given that everyone who seeks therapy has a first time, it's rather surprising that there is so little literature available to prepare folks for the initial session, or what is referred to as the *intake session*. This book is intended as a primer for those curious about or new to therapy.

Most therapists make every effort to help new clients feel safe and at ease. Yet, our would-be clients may have no idea that their comfort level is our priority from the start. Indeed, many clients come in because they feel discomfort, including various forms of anxiety. So if you're considering beginning therapy, it makes sense that you might like to have a thorough description of what to expect before you even arrive. Hopefully, this book will help you overcome any apprehension you might have, so you can enjoy the benefits of therapy with less fear of the unknown. Therapy is meant to remove your worries and soothe your soul. Let's begin that process now—before you even walk through the door.

Your relationship with your therapist is truly special and unique. Even though you'll likely develop an easy rapport and eventual trust, this interaction is unlike a typical social or familial relationship. The unspoken rule of polite reciprocity: you tell me your struggles, I'll tell you mine, does not apply in the therapeutic relationship. When you share, what you share will be explored to your satisfaction. Yes, it really is all about you. And it should be. After all, you're paying for it and you're well worth it. Imagine speaking freely about yourself and your issues with someone engaged, trained, knowledgeable and non-judgmental. Given the container of safety, professionalism and confidentiality, you have the luxury of speaking your truth, hopes, doubts and dreams, with an interested and educated partner. Don't expect them to give unsolicited advice or attempt to fix everything for you. They are there to hold space for your process and guide you along, as you tap into your inner wisdom and move towards more clarity, peace, and happiness.

After Jay shares a thorough history and he and Margaret identify some troublesome relationship patterns and areas for growth, he asks, "So, what happens from here? Is it a weekly thing?" Margaret and Jay agree that meeting weekly for 50 minutes is a good rhythm for now, and decide on a recurring day and time. He provides his credit card to cover the fee and she answers any last questions he has and wraps it up on time. "One more thing," she adds on his way out. "If I see you out and about in town, I won't approach you, so don't think I'm being aloof. I just want to protect your privacy." He looks intrigued and a little surprised. "Oh, okay, that's cool. I appreciate that." He nods with the recognition that yes, this relationship is different. It's designed to be discreet and guard his dignity. "Understood. I won't be offended if you don't introduce yourself to my friend at Starbuck's," he jokes. They share a laugh. "See you next week," he says and turns to leave. He feels relaxed—

even cheerful, at having taken this step for himself. His
therapist is pleased to know that they have begun
building a rapport—the foundation on which his healing
will be based. Yes, it's a unique relationship. Some might
even say, sacred.

A Few Things About This Book

This book is intended to be short, practical and easy to read.
Deciding whether to do therapy needn't add to your stress. If
you're curious enough to read this, you may as well give it a go.
Once you decide to try it, prepping for your first session should
be a breeze. While this book is brief, it's meant to contain everything you generally need to know before stepping into a
psychotherapy session for the first time. By the time you finish
it, you'll have a good idea of what to expect and how to get the
most out of your treatment. That said, therapists and their
approaches and styles vary, so you'll want to keep an open mind.
There is no way to account for every scenario that may arise.
Many variables comprise each situation, including geography, a
client's reason for seeking therapy, the qualifications and
methods of a given therapist, and the dynamic specifics of a
given case. Examples could be described as typical, but this
book, while practical, cannot cover the total breadth of all
possible experiences that may be encountered.

This book is meant to help the prospective therapy client
know what to expect and get the most out of treatment. It's
written for the lay person with the disclaimer that it is not meant
to be an exhaustive, legally precise manual. Legal and ethical
matters are subject to change and vary broadly from professional
license to license and state to state. Furthermore, the author is a
psychotherapist and not an attorney. This book is not written
from a legal standpoint. It's intended to make therapy accessible

to everyone, but cannot attempt to cover all the legal and ethical issues. For information about professional standards of care, please look up current laws in your area, whenever there is a question or concern. The basics of a typical therapeutic situation are covered within these pages, but be prepared for nuances. Therapists are as different as the clients they see. That means there's a therapist out there for you.

If you're someone who functions mostly well in life, despite some challenges or opportunities for growth, this material may be for you. However, it is not appropriate for everyone, including those in immediate distress or crisis. (See insert below.) It's also not inclusive of therapy sessions done electronically or virtually, often referred to as telehealth. Technology continues to impact the field of psychotherapy, just as it changes the world, yet what's relevant today may be obsolete tomorrow. Some of what's covered may apply generally to burgeoning modes of therapy, but what's in these pages is best suited for those who are inclined to do much of their therapy in person.

A Word About Crisis

Typically, psychotherapy is a gradual healing process —not an emergency intervention. It's wonderful to have a therapist to mitigate symptoms, monitor progress and/or process a crisis or trauma, but it's not typical to depend on their help between sessions. When there is an immediate emergency, as always, go to your nearest hospital emergency room or dial 911. A therapist offers support over the long haul, and most are not on call. You can ask your therapist what to do in the event of a crisis. Different therapists may handle this differently. In the United States, 24-hour hotlines such as the SAMHSA Treatment Referral Helpline at 1-800-622-HELP(4357) and the National Suicide Prevention Lifeline at 1-800-273-8255 are available, as well as local resources. Some therapists may be able to see you on short notice, but for private practice clinicians, that most likely cannot be counted on. If you are at risk, contact emergency services immediately. You can always include your therapist once you are out of imminent danger.

Because clients and therapists come in all genders, it doesn't seem appropriate to write in a voice particular to one. It can get confusing when pronouns are switched with every new section or chapter to attempt balance. However, assigning a male or female gender for either therapist or client feels forced. To encompass everyone, you'll encounter the pronoun, "They." Grammatically, it's not ideal to be married to a plural pronoun, but it seems better than the alternatives. Please forgive any awkwardness in language, in favor of inclusivity.

Additionally, please be aware that examples in this book protect the identity of their subjects. When illustrating a case, any identifying information of those involved has been altered in multiple ways. Therapists take client confidentiality extremely seriously. The examples you read in this book have been thoroughly obscured and altered to that end. Examples may draw upon real cases and be fictionalized to provide colorful illustrations without rendering a person recognizable. In some cases, an amalgam of different cases are woven together into a story to illuminate important points while protecting confidentiality.

Other examples included in this book may draw upon my own experiences as a client. Although it may seem counterintuitive, those who know therapy well have typically experienced it first-hand. For those who teach psychology and certainly for those who practice psychotherapy clinically, it's normal and expected to "do one's own work." In higher learning institutions, a minimum number of hours of psychotherapy may be a mandatory requirement for students before a degree is conferred. Why? Because you don't want someone who hasn't thoroughly explored their own inner world, uncovered their blind spots, and worked through their issues projecting their unresolved material onto you. That's not only unprofessional, it's downright dangerous. You deserve a seasoned expert who has done their own therapy as part of their rigorous requirements, and who is qualified to help others. If you were going to take your car to a body shop, would you trust a guy whose own car was all banged up? In addition, I hope to normalize the experience of therapy by being open about my experiences as a client as well as a therapist. The stories relayed in this book are true, although therapists' identities, like clients' identities, are altered to protect privacy.

This book, like therapy, is really all about you. To hit the ground running, skip straight to Chapter One. If you're wondering who I am to talk about starting therapy, here's a bit of context. My designation as a Licensed Marriage and Family Therapist in California (#92539) is part of the reason I could be considered qualified to write on this topic. My enthusiasm in favor of therapy for pretty much everyone, myself included, is another. After an initial career in advertising, I decided to pursue something more meaningful to me. Meaning came first with motherhood, as I was blessed with two awesome sons. While raising them, I went back to school to study a profession that seemed to value peace more than prizes—psychotherapy. Along the way, I did some therapy myself. The truth is, I love therapy—giving it and getting it. I love it for what it can do for those who are wise enough to sign up for the adventure. I love it for doing what friendship cannot. I love it for how it helps me to know myself and how it allows me, as the therapist, to help others know themselves. I find it a wonder—this profession that I'm grateful for and passionate about.

In the pages to come, my positive regard for the therapy profession will be obvious. But here's a bit about why I've appreciated receiving therapy, as well. For one thing, I find it healing, empowering and clarifying to say everything without owing anything (other than payment) in return. For another, I've been through stuff, like everyone else. It feels really good to clean that stuff up, as needed. Lastly, I'm a personal-growth devotee, which means that my internal examination is never-ending.

My experience as a client informs my expertise on therapy every bit as much as my experience as a clinician. The investment we make in psychological self-awareness benefits everyone whose lives we touch. As mentioned before, we therapists know that you don't want a therapist who has not done their own therapy. Having gone to various therapists myself with differing results, I know what can go right or wrong on the couch as well as from the chair. I hope that what comes through on these pages is enhanced by my reverence for therapy from both sides of the room.

LET'S TALK ABOUT THERAPY

Therapy is a term that is broadly applied to many methods of healing. You've probably heard of speech therapy, massage therapy and hypnotherapy, to name a few. There are many types of therapy available to address specific concerns. In general, therapy is a curative process engaged to heal a symptom or solve a problem. This book will focus is on a particular type of therapy known as psychotherapy, which is also commonly referred to as counseling. Psychotherapy addresses psychological concerns and promotes mental well-being. Often, it is simply referred to as therapy. To be clear, where it says therapy within these pages, it is referring to psychotherapy and not some other type.

There are many definitions of psychotherapy. What follows is a general description, intended to give you a basic grasp of what to expect when you begin. Generally, psychotherapy addresses concerns you might have about how you think, feel or act. Through a process of relating with a trained professional, your licensed psychotherapist, you are able to gain awareness and understanding of yourself, your life and your relationships, and initiate positive changes towards greater health and happiness.

When it comes to therapy, there is no cookie cutter experience. Each client is different, each therapist is different, and the objectives in any given case are different. Pretty much anything you can think of is fair game to address in therapy, because therapy addresses your internal world, which is infinite. If you're thinking it, feeling it, or doing it, you can share about it in session. You can even share about how you feel about your session in session, real time, as it's unfolding. Please do! This is good information for you and your therapist. Dr. Keven Pinjuv, PhD, tells all his clients at the start, "One thing that is so important is that you feel that you can comment on therapy itself. If you ever have feelings about how it's going, if you are skeptical, or annoyed or happy or whatever, please do let me know. It can be strange but it really does help us pivot in a way that will make this more helpful."

When you offer feedback about how therapy is going, it will be taken to heart. Your therapist is in a better position to help you when they know what works for you. Yet even if they do everything to your liking, how well therapy works for you will be up to you. Even if you find yourself the perfect therapist, the gains made will be yours to make. When you're committed to your therapy, you will get the most out of it. The good news is, you don't have to do it all alone. When the going gets tough (even just a little tough), your psychotherapist will be there as a partner on your path to progress. As will be emphasized repeatedly, this is not a friendship. It is a professional alliance forged on your behalf. Therapy is a relational path to healing initiated by you, for you. Your therapist provides a safe space for you to examine yourself and your mental and emotional experiences without judgment. Even though psychotherapy is intended to bring some relief, it's not up to your therapist to fix everything for you.

At the core, therapy involves talking to your psychotherapist about what's on your mind and in your heart. Sometimes, a therapist will begin by asking you what you want to "work on." Don't let the term "work" turn you off. They probably just want a sense of what to focus on, so your time is dedicated towards your highest good, with your particular goals in mind. Whether that actually feels like "work," or you find that you enjoy yourself, or you land somewhere in between, will vary from person to person and session to session. It depends on you, the content you explore and the unique dynamic between you and your therapist. Rest assured—a therapist is trained to make you feel at ease. Their first priority is to build a rapport with you.

Not much can happen unless you feel that you are comfortable, safe, and with someone you can really trust. How quickly and completely you trust your therapist varies from person to person. Some people are cautious, or hesitant to reveal themselves until some time has passed. Others are an open book from the start. Trust, and the timing of it, are on a spectrum. Your willingness to share of yourself may correlate to the amount of trust you have, whether that comes quickly or over time. At a minimum, your therapist has to be that someone you can talk to when it's time to "talk to someone." So, the first order of business is to establish a connection based on empathy, understanding and mutual respect. Once that's in place, you can explore freely and be real with yourself and your therapist. The more honest and open you are, the more you can expect improvement. Just like most things worth doing, you get out what you put in. Pace and duration of therapy will be addressed by you and your therapist together in the beginning and as needed.

Just as every therapist and client are different, no therapist works exactly the same way. There are many approaches to therapy, which will not be covered in this short book. It may take a little curiosity on your part to get into the specifics of a therapist's theoretical orientation. If your therapist was trained as a Jungian Analyst, for example, you may want to ask what that means and how it informs their work. Many clients aren't concerned with a therapist's background or areas of expertise, but it may benefit you to know. Some offer a specific type of therapy, such as CBT (cognitive behavioral therapy), while others have an eclectic approach, employing relevant aspects of various methods, as appropriate.

Even when two therapists have a similar approach, they will still have a personal style. For example, two therapists who deem themselves "client-centered" may differ in how directive they are with clients. Client-centered is a term from the Humanistic School of Psychotherapy, which means the therapist pays attention to the client's style and preferences, given that they know best what works for them. (More on this in a bit). But even amongst therapists who have this perspective, there will be variation. Does the therapist sit back and mostly listen? Or do they interact and offer insights and ideas often? What kind of approach works best for you—a more passive therapist or a more interactive one? Ultimately, it's up to you to discern whether the dynamic between you and a given therapist is a good fit. You're the customer. Ask questions. Be choosey.

What Might Lead a Person to Seek Therapy?

From playful curiosity to personal crisis, people embark upon therapy for a range of reasons that may arise at any stage of life. It's worth repeating that therapy does not imply one is mentally ill. It may in fact indicate that one is so well that they notice even the slightest imbalance and seek to investigate and correct it at first notice. Seeking therapy doesn't have the stigma it once had. In general, it's an accepted form of self-care. Of course, there are exceptions to every rule. If you're in a situation where you may be investigated or scrutinized by an employer, for example, you may want to consider whether receiving therapy could be a liability somehow. If you're concerned, ask your potential therapist to clarify the limits of confidentiality as they apply in your unique circumstances.

In most cases, your decision to seek therapy will be between you, your therapist and those whom you choose to tell. Some folks don't disclose they're in therapy beyond their intimate circle. Others speak freely about it, without any hesitation. These days, therapy is commonly part of a wellness regimen. When you say you're seeing a therapist, you're sending a message that you take care of yourself. That kind of self-care is a healthy model for others. Enlisting help in any area of life as needed is a good idea. Reaching out to a therapist is no different. If you need a little help from time to time, don't hesitate to get it. Life transitions, stages of life, relationships and personal growth apply to everyone. Typical life stuff can be reason enough to do a course of therapy. When clients approach me, I have immediate respect for them. Reaching out is a sign of strength, resilience, humility, intelligence, hope and responsibility.

There may be a general or specific need that drives one's decision to embark upon therapy. Particular symptoms may be bothering you. For example, maybe you don't like the way you feel lately. Maybe your unchecked thoughts are causing distress, leading to anxiety or depression. Or perhaps you're ready to break old patterns or habits that no longer serve you, such as out-of-control anger, obsession with body-image or substance abuse. These are all good reasons to seek therapy, yet there are countless others. You might go based on a feeling or just from simple curiosity. Often, challenges that arise in relationships drive folks to therapy. Dating, intimacy, partnerships and commitment pose challenges for all of us. Family of origin is a common catalyst for therapy as well. In some cases, old familial roles or wounds need to be understood and overcome.

Trauma is another good reason to seek treatment. Traumas come in all shapes and sizes. Whether you stumbled into a wasp's nest, got bullied in middle-school, or survived a plane crash, it's trauma. Any intense experience that leaves a lingering negative effect in its wake can be traumatic—an accident, a death, abuse, unfair treatment, witnessing tragedy, humiliation, perceived failure, loss, a breakup, or any moment when life hits you hard. If your nervous system is still activated, or what's often called *triggered,* treatment may help. Put simply, if you're still disruptively bothered now by what happened back then, therapy could bring the relief you seek.

Phase of life issues may lead one to therapy as well. If we're fortunate enough to have a long life, let's face it, there will likely be some rough patches along the way. Growing up, managing relationships, grieving the loss of loved ones, and "knowing thyself" are common reasons to visit "the couch." A stint of therapy, short or long, may be useful for one stage and revisited in another. For example, a young adult may have anxiety over leaving home to go far away for college. With the support of his parents, he seeks therapy as a young adult, to overcome fears and feel confident about his path forward. Later in life, he may seek therapy again with his fiancé, for some pre-marital counseling to get on solid footing with his partner before the big day. He may revisit therapy a decade later, to manage the stress of parenting a defiant child or to work on anger management. Perhaps you can see how one might seek out therapy as an individual, a couple, a family, or even a group, depending on the challenge and the dynamics involved.

The recognition that "something's not right here… it's time for a change," demonstrates resilience. Believe it or not, saying, "Help!" is a sign of strength. Self-awareness, too, can be an indication of sound mental health. When someone takes responsibility for their part in a destructive relational dynamic, for example, that is a sign of maturity, humility and honest self-reflection. If they're able to admit they have a problem and express a desire to change, the decision to do something about it benefits all the people around them as well. It is generous to work on yourself, even as it rewards you the most.

Although this book is generally intended for individual adult clients, there are many kinds of therapy. In addition to individual therapy, there are other common client configurations as well, such as child, family and couples therapy. In general, a legal guardian (typically a parent or parents) will initiate the process of therapy for a child, consenting for their treatment and taking care of paperwork and payment on their behalf. A young adult may be able to consent to their own treatment, depending on the circumstances and whether they are legally old enough to do so in their given state. If a family or couple is embarking on therapy, they generally all go together to each session. If you're interested in learning more about therapy for children, couples or families, you may want to seek out more information beyond these pages. That said, many of the general guidelines you'll find here still apply, with some modifications.

What if you're interested in therapy but puzzled by whether you need therapy? What if you think you may benefit but you're not sure? Keep in mind that the simple quest for self-knowledge is reason enough. In fact, it's a noble pursuit. You do not need a list of acute symptoms to justify beginning therapy, but you will need motivation and curiosity. Sometimes, folks go into a first session expecting to work on one thing and realize that there is a more pressing issue to process. That happens. We can't predict the course of a session. Every process unfolds in its own way and in its own time.

If you have a desire to try therapy but you're not sure exactly what your "goals" would be—that's just fine. You can explore that in the course of your treatment at any point if you so choose. One of the most rewarding things about being a human being is engaging in the inner journey. How well do you know yourself? How much do you like and love yourself? How happy can you be? And then there are the age-old existential questions, like

"What is the meaning of life? What's my purpose? What about death?" These topics are well suited for exploration in therapy. If you want to understand yourself better and examine your life, that's reason enough to engage in the eye-opening, mind-expanding, life-affirming adventure of psychotherapy.

A Short History of Therapy

For those interested in the history of psychology and psychotherapy, plentiful information is available in books, articles and online. Many brilliant visionaries have made significant contributions to the field. This partial overview highlights just a few, to give you a bit of historical context. You may be fascinated to learn more beyond this glimpse.

The field of psychology is considered to be relatively young. Early influences come from philosophers like Aristotle and Plato and scientists like Charles Darwin. In 1879, Wilhelm Wundt, a physician and professor, launched the first psychological laboratory in Germany. Wundt is known as the father of psychology and the first to call himself a psychologist. His experiments focused on the mind, including thoughts, consciousness and introspection.

In the 1880s, Sigmund Freud famously brought attention to the unconscious mind. He emphasized dreams, aspects of the ego (id/ego/superego), repressed drives, childhood memories and sexuality. As a departure from hypnosis, which Freud had practiced, he pioneered psychoanalysis, a method of making unconscious material conscious by engaging in an alliance between the analysist and his subject. The invention of "talk therapy" may more accurately be accredited to Freud's lesser known mentor, Josef Breuer.

Following these formative breakthroughs came a steady stream of new approaches to therapy. Although Freud's contribution is well known, many theories that followed diverged from his emphasis. During the early 1900s, various fresh approaches were introduced and embraced. Alfred Adler left psychoanalysis to practice his own type of therapy, called Individual Psychology. Carl Jung also parted ways with Freud to include spirituality in his form of analysis. The mid-twentieth century ushered in the birth of Behaviorism, based on the work of scientist B.F. Skinner, which eventually led to the development of Cognitive Behavioral Therapy (CBT), a common form of treatment today. Another important development happened in the 1950s with the rise of Humanism, based on the work of Carl Rogers, Abraham Maslow and others. Humanistic psychology popularized the notion of human potential and self-actualization as a worthy pursuit.

As the field of psychotherapy evolved, there was an important shift in how the customer is regarded, from a framework of pathology to one of wellness. In the early days, psychoanalysis followed from hypnosis, where a "patient" might lie down on a couch and let the "doctor" lead. These sessions had an inherently hierarchical dynamic. That is, the psychotherapist was considered the superior expert and the patient assumed a subordinate role. Fortunately, these antiquated clichés no longer apply.

Carl Rogers' pivotal work, *Client-Centered Therapy* (1951), offered a refreshing and optimistic paradigm shift. He proposed that people should be treated as clients, or customers, rather than patients. Both of importance to the other, clinicians and clients would collaborate to direct the course of therapy according to the unique specifics of each client and their case. This approach to therapy assumes an automatic respect for the client and their ability to know what works, what doesn't, and how the course of treatment will best unfold. This premise of mutual respect is a hallmark of most schools of psychotherapy today and one embraced wholeheartedly in this book.

Many developments have occurred since the 1950s, and new approaches continue to be introduced. If you're interested in the history of a theoretical orientation, do your research and/or ask your therapist. Regardless of nuances, chances are, the basic ingredients of therapy will be in place, respect for you among them.

Training for Therapists

Training for therapists is incredibly important. In the United States, it is not legal or ethical to practice counseling or therapy without proper education, training and a license. When considering a therapist, be aware of the particular title they use and make sure it's backed up with a license number to match. For example, a psychologist, a marriage and family therapist, or social worker should have a license number visible on promotional materials and online. Many people would like to call themselves counselors and therapists. However, unlike other fields such as life coaching or spiritual guidance, which have ethical standards but not legal requirements per se, a psychotherapist without ample training and current licensure is not permitted to practice therapy.

The requirements for therapists vary, depending on the type of license earned and the state where one practices. In general, however, mandatory coursework, a practicum and/or internship of supervised hours of experience, as well as a minimum of therapy for the aspiring therapist are required. In addition, clinicians are expected and required to engage in ongoing continuing education, to ensure their skills and training stay up-to-date. Without training, people quite naturally fall into "fixing," or correcting people's beliefs, and—even more dangerous—they can fall into abusive behaviors. The rigors of a career in counseling or psychotherapy are in place for good reason—to protect their clients and ensure the highest standard of care.

There are many titles and types of licenses that may describe a therapist's qualifications. What follows is just an overview of some of the mental healthcare professionals who might be considered qualified to offer therapy. If you have any doubt that you're in the hands of a trained professional, ask your therapist about their qualifications. It's perfectly alright to ask what kind of education, training and license they have. You deserve the assurance that your inner world is being trusted to a skilled professional.

Because the term therapy is used in a broad and generic sense, it can be confusing to know whether a clinician is properly credentialed or not. Getting unpaid advice is one thing, but paying for therapy is another. Although it's not okay for someone unqualified to practice therapy, that doesn't mean it doesn't happen. For example, healers, teachers or practitioners of other kinds may offer something different ostensibly, yet in the course of your work together, the content of your sessions goes outside the boundaries of the arrangement and they slip into "doing therapy." This isn't fair to you, because they are not trained and seasoned enough to safely know what they're doing. Nor is it fair to therapists who take the profession seriously and dedicate themselves to meeting the stringent requirements to practice. Even if someone seems to know what they're doing, it's best to be sure. Licensed therapists are trained to do no harm. If you're disclosing your deepest personal truth, that ought to give you peace of mind. One way to ensure you're in capable hands is to look at the type of license your therapist has earned. If you see something like PsyD, LMFT or LCSW next to their name, for example, that's a good sign. But what do those letters mean?

Here's a brief, partial look at some legitimate designations for therapists. Titles and license types may differ depending on where you live. If you have any question about the type of qualifications a given therapist has, ask away and do some research. Your peace of mind is in everyone's best interest. Most mental health professionals have dedicated many years to schooling and clinical practice and have passed rigorous testing to be able to work with you. They will most likely be more than happy to share about their hard-earned credentials.

You may have heard terms like psychiatrist, psychologist, counselor, social worker and psychotherapist. All of these professionals may offer therapy—so what's the difference? Generally, education, hours of clinical experience and licensing exams are required. However, specific requirements differ depending on the license and certification earned. A psychiatrist is a medical doctor specializing in mental health. These physicians have had medical school, residency and testing to attain a medical license and board certification. Psychiatrists manage medication and may also do varying degrees of therapy with their patients. Given their training and expertise, psychiatrists tend to charge much more than other therapists, so it's not commonly practical or financially feasible to see them for weekly sessions. If that's the case, a psychiatrist may refer a patient to a therapist for therapy, while they continue to check in less frequently and manage medication. Conversely, if you begin therapy with another type of therapist and they believe a medical evaluation for medication is in your best interest, they may refer you to a psychiatrist as they continue to see you as well.

Psychologists are also called doctors because they have attained a psychology degree at the doctoral level, although they do not prescribe medication because they are not medical doctors. They may focus on psychological testing, research, clinical practice or some combination of these. Psychologists are typically designated with the letters PhD or PsyD.

Master's Degree level therapists come with many titles. Some typical designations include Marriage and Family Therapist, Clinical Social Worker, Mental Health Counselor or School Counselor, among others. These therapists have attained a master's degree in psychology and, like psychologists, they have attained many mandatory hours of clinical experience (often around 3,000 hours) and passed rigorous exams to attain their license. The actual work these therapists do may look very similar in practice, although each may approach therapy from a slightly different angle. For example, Licensed Marriage and Family Therapists (LMFT or MFT) are thought to have a relational focus. If you are interested in family of origin work, couples counseling, or parenting help, for example, these relationship dynamics are a focus for LMFTs.

Clinical Social Workers also have knowledge of relationships, but may have an emphasis on day-to-day functioning in various environments, as well. An LCSW (Licensed Clinical Social Worker) is trained to consider the context of one's life situation and how that impacts wellness. They are known to go into homes and work environments to assess functioning, in addition to providing counseling, for example. That said, therapists and counselors, regardless of specialties, are typically qualified to work with a range of people and a myriad of issues.

As long as your therapist is officially credentialed and licensed, the only question that remains is fit. Ultimately, your therapeutic gains depend upon a comfortable, trusting relationship between you and your therapist. If for any reason you don't feel you can share openly with them after a reasonable break-in period, you may want to look elsewhere for help, regardless of the letters by their name. A psychotherapist may have an impressive title, an air of prestige and a high fee to match, but none of that matters if you can't say what you need to say in their presence over time. By the same token, someone who's overly friendly and casual may be off putting as well, if you don't feel enough respect for them as a professional to be well served. If you find yourself in a Goldilocks predicament, keep looking. You'll find a therapist who feels just right and you'll probably gain plenty of self-knowledge along the way. That said, if you don't imagine yourself feeling super comfortable in a therapeutic setting, regardless of the therapist, then you may want to stick with it for a few sessions and give it a chance. Some people have a harder time being vulnerable and intimately honest with people in general, for their own good reasons. If you have a hunch you'd feel squirmy or avoidant no matter who's in the therapist's chair, then you may do well to hang in there and see how a therapist works for you over time. The truth is, sometimes even the "wrong" therapist can prompt the right results for you. Therapy works in mysterious ways. You'll learn about yourself based on what works, what doesn't, and how much you share about that along the way. Indeed, therapists are ready for your feedback and welcome it. They're prepared to hear your skepticism about therapy when it arises, and talking about it is part of the process.

Shawn, a 31-year-old male, arrived to his session visibly exasperated. As he sat down, he began to vent his frustrations, one after the other. "I'm never gonna get any work done with my mother visiting. She drives me crazy. Every time I open my laptop, she interrupts me. It's so annoying!" Shawn altered his voice to imitate his mother: *How do I turn on the TV again? I forget which remote goes to the cable...Now you're not going to make me watch* Master Chef *all alone are you?* Shawn went on like this for about 10 minutes. Then he paused.

After listening carefully, his therapist, Jennifer, gently offered a suggestion. "I understand your frustration, Shawn. That's a tricky situation." Shawn nodded silently. "I wonder, have you considered suggesting she stay at a hotel? There are loving ways to initiate that conversation with her...?" Shawn glared at Jennifer and looked away, shaking his head. "Not helpful!" he barked.

After taking a moment to regain composure, he apologized. "I'm sorry, it's just...the last thing I need right now is obvious advice." Although Jennifer knew her response hadn't been received well, she had gained valuable information about Shawn and his needs in therapy.

The silver lining came when Shawn and Jennifer talked openly about their uncomfortable exchange immediately afterward. Shawn confessed that he was shocked by how curt he'd been towards her. Jennifer asked if perhaps her suggestion may have seemed "stupid," like much of what he'd been hearing from his mother lately. A light bulb went on for Shawn. Yes, her response had registered as stupid, because he'd already mulled over exactly what she'd suggested and ruled it out. He hadn't taken the time to explain this to Jennifer or why he believed it wouldn't work. Furthermore, he could see how he'd transferred his frustration with his mother onto his therapist. This made him realize that he'd been projecting his discontent with his mother onto his girlfriend, unintentionally, as well.

How to Find a therapist

So, you're ready to give therapy a try but don't know where to start? Finding the right therapist can be a process. Approach the exploration with an open mind. You may be fortunate to find just the right person right away. Beginner's luck applies with therapy remarkably often. That said, it's perfectly OK to shop around as needed. If you have mixed feelings, that's totally normal. You can decide whether working with this therapist is worth exploring further or not. Just know that the interpersonal dynamic between you is the most important consideration. Who will you honor with the official green light to explore the depths of your mind and soul?

If you get a word-of-mouth referral or do a little internet research beforehand, you're more likely to get a good fit right

off the bat. Although for many the first time's a charm, it's
perfectly normal to have an initial session with more than one
therapist, before you commit to subsequent sessions. Nothing is
more important than the fit between you and your qualified therapist. If something is in the way of you fully revealing yourself
over time, consider whether that can be overcome, or whether
you need to keep looking. It's important to like your therapist,
but this is very different than a friendship. The real question is,
do you trust them enough? Will you be able to unveil yourself
of any usual masks so you can be totally real in the presence of
this person? Ask yourself this question: *Can I tell them
anything?*

The answer to that question doesn't have to be 100% yes,
right off the bat. It may take some time to feel comfortable
enough to share deep or personal material. Some things might be
easy to reveal. Others might take months or even a year or more
to disclose. The process and pace of unfolding is ultimately up to
you. Your therapist can guide you, but you're in charge. If you
feel reasonably comfortable and safe, that's a good beginning.
As you develop trust over time, you may forget about filtering
and speak more and more freely.

Granted, in the beginning you will be relying on your gut
instinct about who's right for you. It's a bit like dating. You
might get a feel for someone from an online presence, text or
call, but the real test of a good match comes when you actually
meet. The more you spend time with your therapist, the more
you can tell if it's a relationship worth cultivating. You may want
to have a brief phone call with a few different therapists to get a
feel for what they're like and how they work, if they're willing
to do so. Some therapists don't engage in calls prior to the first
session. They presumably have good reasons for this. For example, they may believe that the only way to really get a sense of
each other is in person. Or they may not want to interact without
a consent form in place. Don't be afraid to ask what's customary

for a given therapist. It varies. In some cases, a free consultation session may be an option.

Your long-term gains ought to make it well worth the initial investment of shopping around. So how do you get the names of a few therapists to try? Old fashioned word-of-mouth is a great way to go, if someone you know and trust has a referral for you. A first-hand endorsement could short-cut your search. This can get tricky, however, if the referral source is someone close to you or someone you see often. Keep in mind that you'll want to be able to tell your therapist anything and speak freely about anything and anyone. What you each say will be confidential, but might the knowledge that you share a therapist create an awkward situation for you at some point down the road? For example, if you start individual therapy with the same person your girlfriend sees, and in a few weeks you two have a big fight, will you feel awkward seeking help from the same person she does? If you break up, does one of you keep the therapist? Do you both? While family and friends may be a great referral source, consider whether the overlap would be a factor in your ability to fully disclose.

A more distant contact, such as an acquaintance or colleague, may be able to point you in the right direction. If someone you know less intimately raves about their therapist, you could ask whom they see, if you feel comfortable doing that. Of course, a therapist that's perfect for one person is not necessarily right for you, so keep an open mind and decide for yourself. Some people are vocal about their love of therapy and eager to share contact information. Others may be discreet. Word-of-mouth referrals are wonderful when you can get them. Even if you don't want to pursue therapy just yet, make a note of any therapists who earn raves from their clients for a later date. You never know who might need them someday—maybe even you.

If you don't know anyone who is doing therapy or openly talking about it, consider asking someone you respect in a professional capacity. Perhaps a doctor, a person from your spiritual or religious community or a student or teacher in a school psychology department can offer a good referral. You may also have access to a list of recommended therapists at your place of work, through an employee assistance program or human resources department. Think about any possible untapped services that might be available to support you, like a school counseling department, a university campus student resources office, or a health services division of any institution. It's worth asking, "Are any therapy services available? Or do you have any recommendations, if not?"

If you plan to go through your insurance, you may be able to get a list of in-network providers by calling the number on your insurance card or going to their website. This can save you a lot of time, since many therapists do not take insurance. Insurance companies commonly require therapists to submit a diagnosis and/or treatment plan. Be aware of what your insurance company will require your therapist to provide, as this may impact your privacy. If you end up choosing a therapist who is out of network, which is very common, they may be willing to provide an invoice, or "superbill," which you can submit for reimbursement. It all depends on the therapist and the insurance plan, so find out what you need to know before going in. It's best to get clarification on fees, payment and insurance policy before embarking on therapy, so you can rule out scenarios that are unworkable. You will have a broader range of choice if you're willing to pay out of pocket, but that is an individual decision, depending upon you and your budget.

The internet is another way to search for therapists. You can do a general search for a psychotherapist in your area or find a site that lists verified professionals according to zip code and region, such as PsychologyToday.com. Therapists typically must pay to be included on these aggregate internet listings, so they are not necessarily comprehensive, although they may be very convenient. You may also enter a specialty that's of interest in your internet search engine, such as couples counseling, anger management or anxiety, to name just a few. While doing your research, you may find that there is a seemingly endless array of things that can lead a person to seek therapy. It may also be reassuring to realize that, whatever you might be facing, you are not alone.

If you already have the name of a therapist, visit their website (if they have one) and see what you can find out. Therapists sometimes keep a low profile online, which is not necessarily a red flag. If you want to give them a try anyway, you may be pleasantly surprised. If not, move on. When searching online, keep in mind that finding a therapist is a more discreet process than other service provider searches. The app that leads you to a 4.5-star restaurant, for example, is not likely to offer an accurate rating of therapists. One reason is that it is unethical for mental health providers to solicit reviews. Asking clients to publically offer positive feedback is problematic and potentially injurious for many reasons. Consider the strict boundaries of confidentiality inherent in this arrangement, for one. Another danger is potential abuse of authority if any kind of favor is asked from a therapist of a client. If you can't find your therapist's ratings and ranking, don't be surprised—many therapists refuse to participate for good reason, with the best interests of their clients in mind.

Thanks to technology, new advances that make it easy to match yourself with a good therapist are being developed. There is clearly a need for more fast and reliable ways to find the right therapist, so be on the lookout for new offerings as they arise. Because beneficial results depend on dynamic live contact, there's not a simple algorithm to get you matched up with the right clinician. However, more websites and apps continue to crop up. Investigate and see what resources are available on the platform you prefer.

Once you've determined a therapist is of interest, consider whether a phone call or email consultation prior to your first session is possible and appropriate. In some cases, your first exchange may have to wait until you arrive at your first session. Some therapists will not talk with clients until papers have been signed, to secure your confidentiality, etc. However, many therapists will engage briefly prior to a first session, over email or phone, to assess fit. If that's the case, you may want to have a list of a few questions ready to go. Be mindful of what you disclose and don't expect a free therapy session. You're really just establishing whether to set up a first appointment. Based upon their experience and expertise, are they well equipped to address your needs?

Notice how you feel during the initial conversation with a potential therapist. If you have a specific objective going into therapy, share about that during your initial contact. For example, if you're seeking help with marital problems, does this therapist see couples? Or if you're looking for therapy because of an addiction, is that something they are trained to address? There are specialists for a seemingly endless array of concerns. If your issue is not within their scope of competence, they may well have a referral or two for you. Don't be afraid to ask, *"Do you know anyone with that specialty that you would recommend?"*

At the first point of contact, assess whether the therapist's style meshes with yours. The process of choosing a therapist engages your intuition and gut instinct, along with your logical discernment. As you cover the bases of availability, specialties, training and fees, notice your level of comfort. Like any new relationship, it takes time to build trust. But generally, you can tell whether someone draws you in, elicits a pleasant but neutral response, or repels you. Your ability to get the most out of therapy depends upon a good rapport or easy connection. You will learn a lot in the first 10 minutes. Remember, this is not a friendship or romantic relationship. Too much attraction can actually be a reason to rule someone out. If you meet in person, for example, and you feel that the therapist is someone you want to impress, that could hinder your ability to be yourself and reveal your truth. Be honest with yourself from the beginning and rule out anything that might get in the way. If you discover that you have mutual friends, belong to the same community organization or frequent the same place, such as a school or yoga studio, discuss that openly and decide whether it's a conflict.

This relationship, like none other, is created for a sacred purpose: your highest good. It need not be compromised. Keep it clean and simple. You deserve to get the most out of therapy. If you try someone for a few sessions and it's not working, you're free to move on. Before you do, however, consider whether hearing some difficult truth or getting out of your comfort zone may be just what you need. Don't be too quick to bail when the going gets tough. That could be a sign that it's working, not that something is wrong. If you're gently called out, challenged or cajoled into thinking differently, that might be just what you need. It's not about what's easy, it's about what works.

Like relationships in general, lessons are learned. If nothing else, you'll know better what works for you in therapy and what doesn't. Feel free to communicate about this with your therapist as you go, as well. You can discuss how well therapy is working for you at any point in the treatment. Whether it's on track, not working for you or awesome beyond your hopes, it's good feedback for your therapist to know how you're doing. Don't be shy about speaking up. This can clear the air and correct course. Even if you decide not to continue with your chosen therapist for your own good reasons, you will no doubt learn something about yourself and the process of therapy. Through the course of your life, you may try different therapists for different reasons at different phases. You'll likely find that you get one thing from one therapist and something just as valuable but entirely different from the next.

Therapy begins with setting the intention to find just the right therapist for you. Here's a short checklist to keep in mind:

- Is this therapist qualified? (What kind of license do they have? What are their credentials? If it's not easily found, don't be afraid to ask. This is key.)
- Does this work for me logistically? (Are they available when I am? Is the office reasonably close and convenient?)
- Does this work for me financially? (What is their hourly rate? Keep in mind an "hour" is usually 50 minutes). Do they have a sliding scale, if needed? (In some cases, therapists adjust their fee for those who can't afford to pay full fee).
- When applicable, do they take insurance? Are they In-Network for my insurance plan? (If not, are they willing to provide a superbill to submit for reimbursement?)
- Do they have experience with my specific concern? (What are their specialties?)
- Do I trust them? (Can I imagine telling them anything in my own time or will I hold back for some reason?)
- Does their style work for me? (e.g., the amount of listening vs. input they give? The words and questions they choose? The rhythm of sessions? The vibe in the room?)

If you like the answers to most or all these questions, you've probably found yourself a good match. See how it goes in those first appointments and trust your intuition. Nothing ventured, nothing gained. Happy therapist hunting and good luck.

2

PREPARING FOR A SESSION

All types of people go to therapy. How a first session goes depends on you, as well as your therapist. If you're generally talkative and energetic, you will most likely find yourself so as you begin therapy. That works. You may be eager to talk about yourself, without the usual social confines that may have you holding back cautiously and reciprocating politely. If you're a human of few words, that will come to bear in your therapy session, as in life. That's perfectly fine as well. Silence isn't considered awkward, like it may be in a casual conversation. Pauses are a chance to regroup and look inward. Sometimes you need a moment to think. Take your time—there's no rush. Your therapist will be there to guide you if you need help, too. That said, no one will force you to say what you don't want to say.

It's a good idea to go in with an idea about what you most want to cover. Therapy is like most things worth doing—you get out what you put in. In a first session, you're assessing whether you can imagine working with this person and engaging in intimate disclosure once comfortable. It doesn't have to be a deep dive right away.

Although there is no expectation that you know what you're

going to say, you might want to give a little thought to some big questions before you arrive. Why am I seeking therapy now? What do I hope to get out of it? How do I feel? What's working and not working in my life? What parts of myself are calling out for attention? What are my symptoms? What changes am I ready to make? How will I know when I've met my goals? Getting clear on why you're seeking therapy and what you want from it will give your sessions a clarity of focus from the very beginning. But if you can't answer these questions, that's fine too. You'll figure it out in session.

First Things First

Of course, getting there is important. Leave plenty of time to account for parking and finding the right office. Arriving early gives you a chance to clear your head and get centered. It may not be possible every time, but it's nice when you don't have to rush, so you're calm and ready to focus. Where you may wait differs. Some therapists work in a building or section of a building with several other therapists. When this is the case, there is often a common waiting area, where you can sit until your therapist is ready for you. Other clients may be there for the same reason, so discretion and silence are typical in a waiting room. There's often an unspoken respect for one another, which offers a soft gaze and attention to one's own business.

It's best not to knock if you arrive early, because the therapist may still be in session with a prior client. However, if your designated appointment time has passed and the door remains closed, it's okay to knock, unless indicated otherwise. Some therapists may be in a building with other kinds of professionals and businesses and may not have a waiting room for you. In that case, you can wait in the hall, outside, in your car, or anywhere comfortable, where you can take some deep breaths and begin to relax.

Occasionally, therapists practice in a designated section of their home or other space. In some cases, home visits are available.

Find out ahead of time where your therapist works. Scope it out. Is it convenient enough? Does it work with your lifestyle? Find the closest bathroom for future reference. Get the lay of the land. If you are late, you will still be charged for the full session, so try not to miss your minutes. Allow yourself a buffer of 10 or 15 minutes, at least until you know the drill.

So you have found your way to the couch. What then? We'll cover that in the next chapter, *What Happens in a Session*.

What's Written

You can expect to be given a consent form by your therapist to read and sign before you begin. Often forms are provided in advance, so you have time for a thoughtful review. Then you'll be prepared to ask any questions you might have. If forms are not available on your therapist's website or emailed to you, you may want to request they be sent. Although consent forms may include similar information, therapists' paperwork varies. Some consent forms are less than a page in length, while others may be several pages long. Read this document thoroughly, regardless, as it contains important information. Such as: What is the cancelation policy? Are you charged if you cancel 48 hours or 24 hours prior to your scheduled time? What are the limits of confidentiality? Although generally protected, your privacy may be compromised in rare cases, such as in the case of expressed intent to harm oneself or another, or if ordered or required by law. When insurance is used, you will want to understand the extent of information your insurance company is provided. You might want to consider whether having a 3rd party privy to a diagnosis and treatment would have possible ramifications in any way. Exceptions to confidentiality may vary according to the state where you are seeking therapy. You have a right to know the parameters going in, so feel free to ask if you have any questions, before you authorize treatment.

In addition to a customary consent form, some therapists ask for background information prior to or at the start of therapy. They may ask about your history of physical and/or mental illness and/or whether you have any prior experience of therapy, your family history, etc. Like a consent form, a background (or intake form, as it's also called) may vary in length and contain questions according to the discretion of the therapist. While you will generally have a consent form, background forms are less routine. Some therapists gather relevant biographical information in the course of therapy. Apart from these common forms, your therapist may have others. Some therapists are into paperwork. Others, not so much. Regardless, this paper filling-out stuff is typically a one-time thing. Once you've signed any preliminary documents, you will be ready to focus on the talking part of therapy, which is really what it's all about.

As you begin sharing about yourself, your therapist will be ready to listen. Initial sessions tend to include lots of background information, so expect more questions in those first sessions. Some therapists will have a pad of paper at hand, while others may never pick up a pen. Notetaking during a session may vary greatly from therapist to therapist, or even from session to session, and is not an indication of the quality of your treatment. Don't let it stress you out if a therapist takes notes. This is just a stylistic choice which each therapist makes, depending on what works for them. If your therapist captures notes digitally, let them know if that bothers you. It's important to feel that you have their full attention. Of course, typing onto a screen is convenient, but if it's off-putting to you, say so. I once saw a therapist who took notes on his iPad with his feet up throughout our sessions. I was pretty sure he wasn't playing a game or researching his next vacation, but it was a distraction to wonder.

Right or wrong, the screen between us made him seem less attentive and present to me. What style works for you is personal
preference. Just know that therapists differ in manner and
method, and what works for one client may not for another. After
sessions, your therapist will keep any notes or records in confidence, customarily in a locked file cabinet, if any are taken by
hand. If you have any questions or doubt about the security of
your privacy, do ask.

You might want to jot down a few things you'd like to cover
in your session before you start. This is not a must. It's common
to go in and know quite well what you plan to cover without any
reference. But it could help you get the most out of your time.
Rather than telling a story about the unexpected ups and downs
of your day, you can launch into the bigger issue that caused you
to seek therapy. It's ok to give an update, but a laundry list of the
week's events will eat up your 50 minutes quickly. Some therapists may say that any content is relevant. Your presence is informative beyond words. But rather than small talk, consider what
thoughts, feelings, actions or relationships will be most helpful
to share about. "I think I'm sabotaging my relationship with a
really cool person again," is probably a more useful topic than
"I'm watching a Netflix series about..." Unless of course, the
show is relevant to your own life and you're sharing for a good
reason, which could very well be the case. Just be sure to
connect the dots before you find yourself detailing Season 3.

Just as you may bring some bullet points of things you'd like
to share in a given session, you can make a list of goals at the
beginning, to refer back to and stay on track with throughout
your course of treatment. You don't necessarily need a list. In
fact, most clients don't prep to that degree. But if you want to
capture your thoughts, it's a good way to do so. Some therapists
will ask you what your goals for therapy are, others will not.
Either way, it may be helpful for you to get clear with yourself
on that. Ask yourself why you're going, what you hope to get out

of it and how you'll know when you get there. You may also change and add to that list as you go. Therapy is like peeling an onion. If you're invested in personal growth, there's always another layer to explore. That said, you're free to stop when you meet your goals, or continue as you add new ones. Your objectives may evolve as you do.

Another relevant thing you might want to do is to write down your recent or recurring dreams. This can offer an intriguing lens into your unconscious mind. This is by no means a must—it's just another possible source of material to process in session. Since dreams are often hard to remember after you first wake up, it's a good idea to keep a journal or pad of paper at your bedside. Believe it or not, going to bed with the intention to remember your dreams can actually help you remember them. You don't need to recount the whole dream for it to be valuable. Sometimes just an image or a feeling is enough to be curious about and explore. If you like, write down whatever you remember and feel free to bring your notes to your session. Your therapist will most likely not interpret your dream. Rather, they will listen and *help you* to make meaning of the material for yourself. Dreams are a rare and wonderful way for your unconscious mind to communicate to your conscious mind. They can deliver messages or information that you otherwise would not be able to access. That said, it may not come up in therapy unless you bring it up. Some therapists are more apt to ask about your dreams than others. But if something important to you happens, even during sleep, there is little to lose and much to be gained from sharing about it in session.

Pioneers in psychology, Sigmund Freud and Carl Jung, emphasized the importance of dreams. Dreams can serve as a bridge to the unconscious and provide indispensable information that we would not otherwise be able to access. What goes on under the surface, beyond your wakeful awareness? Are you curious? Is there anything to be learned from the material in your dreams? Dream recollection and reflection can lead to insights that you may otherwise miss. Aside from writing about your dreams, you can draw them or express them creatively in your own way. For a beautiful example of a thoughtful and lovingly rendered dream journal spanning many years, see Larry Vigon's book, *Dream, A Journal (Quantuck Lane Press, 2006),* which features his paintings and descriptions of many intriguing dreams, remembered over a 15-year period.

You may want to jot down what you learn or what you forgot to say after a session as well. It's up to you. There is no formula. If you take responsibility for your treatment, you will know when and how much to write, if anything. When assessing your therapist, keep in mind that all things have a beginning. A first session is an indication of what you're signing up for. However, your first few sessions may differ from those you have over time because the beginning tends to be a bit of a data dump. That is, you spend those initials sessions filling in the backstory and getting your therapist up to speed on where you've been, where you are now and where you want to go. Don't go in expecting to have your presenting problem resolved in the first session. Long term benefits aren't typically found immediately. There are types of therapy dedicated to a shorter term of treatment. For example, Brief Therapy offers a more finite timeframe. But instant gratification isn't the norm. Might you have an early "Ah ha" moment, a pivotal insight, or get an indispensable intervention in the very first session? Absolutely. But there's no doubt more to uncover, explore, and learn.

A Peek at Things Legal

Note: Since laws vary state to state and laws change, be sure to get the latest, most accurate information that applies currently where you receive therapy.

Consent Form: Most therapists are obligated to have a

written service agreement with their clients that at a minimum gives consent for the therapist to provide treatment. Many consent forms will also require contact information, briefly describe therapy or the particular approach of this therapist, set out the fees and policies for making appointments, cancellations, and the like. You should review the Consent Form carefully and it should make sense to you. If it is confusing, ask your questions before signing it.

Confidentiality: Many Consent Forms will also talk about client confidentiality, but some therapists will provide a separate form for that. Somewhere it should be clear what the rules of confidentiality are, and in what circumstances information you share with the therapist may not be kept confidential. Therapists are "mandatory reporters" of child or elder abuse which means that if they become aware that a child or elder has been or is at risk of being abused they *must* report that to the appropriate public agency. If one of the concerns leading you to seek therapy involves physical, sexual, or emotional abuse of a minor or elder, your communications about that may require the therapist to make a report. This is an area where you should be thoughtful about what you disclose. Know the rules before going into detail on what you believe to be confidential disclosures.

Another major area of exception to client confidentiality is if you are a danger to yourself or others, or gravely disabled, in which case the therapist may disclose to police or medical authorities for your own safety and that of others. Again, it is best to know the rules prior to making disclosures. Talk about policies with your therapist until you feel comfortable and well informed.

Insurance: If you are intending to use insurance to

pay for or reimburse your therapy costs, the insurance company will be entitled to certain information. It is important for you to know that and also know how the insurance company uses that information, as it may affect your future health insurance or other matters. Insurance companies require a "diagnosis" in order to reimburse for treatment, which may impose a medical or psychological label that has other consequences. Be thoughtful about who will be entitled to information about your therapy so that you are not surprised by disclosure of information you have shared with your therapist.

Background Forms: Some therapists will also ask you to provide some background information in writing, often before the first session. If it is more than contact information, again be aware of limits of confidentiality before sharing sensitive information on a form. If you are uncomfortable with any of the questions or your answers, save those for face-to-face discussion with your therapist. If the therapist is not collecting background information prior to the first session, you can cover that in person and provide any requested paperwork at your initial meeting.

Show Up

When possible, it's a good idea to center yourself before therapy. If you have a chance to catch your breath before going in, you may have more clarity about what you need. This can be done by journaling a bit, meditating or just breathing deeply as you wait. There is no expectation that you are in a Zen state of mind as you embark on your session. It's just a good idea to get calm and clear about your intention for the time before you begin, if and when that's feasible. If not, you can settle yourself once there.

Your therapist can help you do this. Feel free to ask or just take a moment or two to close your eyes, breathe and tune in.

You won't need to bring much when you go to therapy. Your form of payment, a bottle of water, if you like, and notes if you have them. If it's your first session, you might also have your therapist's forms, if they were provided ahead of time. Mainly, you just need to show up. Keep in mind that you are not obligated to continue with this therapist if something feels off. You may be asked whether you'd like to schedule another session or weekly sessions. While it's helpful to be prepared for the question, you don't necessarily have to know the answer on the spot. You may feel sure and want to sign up for more. You may feel sure that you don't. Or you may want to give yourself a few days to decide. Don't worry about offending your therapist if you need some time. Know that, in essence, you're the customer and you're in charge. Unless your therapy is court mandated or there are extreme circumstances, there is no obligation to continue, so don't feel pressured. Be present during your session and then you will be able to discern whether you'd like to continue. Ideally, whatever hesitation you might have about trying therapy will disappear quickly when you're in the right hands.

___

3

WHAT HAPPENS IN A SESSION?

You may have picked up ideas of what therapy is like from books, television shows, or movies. Therapy is sometimes portrayed in a strikingly real way. Other times it is the subject of satire, making for hilarious comedy. If your sense of how therapy works comes from media, read on. Dramatizations may not be accurate, since often artistic liberties are taken.

The Setting

Therapy offices vary as much as therapists do. The furniture, wall and floor coverings, lighting, etc. may be generic, or thoughtfully appointed to create a certain aesthetic. Generally, you'll find a comfy place to sit, a tissue box nearby and maybe a few pillows to make you feel at home. As long as the office space is conveniently located, amenable and welcoming, you should be in a place that lends itself to the process. If there is anything that makes you feel uncomfortable in the environment, take that into consideration. If you're cold or the sun is in your eyes, speak up. Accommodations can often be made, if and when needed. You'll be creating a safe and sacred place with your therapist. It's appropriate to set the stage. That said, a less than lovely atmosphere is hardly a consideration if you find yourself with the right therapist. Ideally, the setting will be a pleasant place you like to visit, where you feel comfortable and at home.

It may be worth mentioning that you can "come as you are" to therapy. Your attire may be casual or formal according to your lifestyle and circumstances. If what you are wearing would pass at the nearest coffee shop, it's most likely fine for your therapy session. Your therapist isn't going to judge you.

Aside from extenuating circumstances, it's a good idea to silence your phone and give your full attention for the hour. Avoid distractions. The only ingredients needed are you, your therapist and a place to sit. There may be times when your therapist employs tools, which we'll touch upon at the end of this chapter. Regardless, you are the main event. Show up and be yourself. This is a place you can go without a mask, so you can relax. Unlike other encounters, this isn't a time to be concerned with appearances. As you begin to feel at ease, you'll be free to reveal what's on the inside.

The Flow of Therapy

Once you find yourself in the right place and say hello, you'll most likely take care of any business first. For example, you can touch base about the calendar, confirm upcoming appointments and do any housekeeping that needs to be addressed. If this is your first session, scheduling may be handled at the end of the session, so you have a chance to confirm that you want to return. Regular appointments are helpful, so your therapist can reserve a time for you. It also helps with your commitment and momentum. You're not obliged to go every week, but it's good to keep an open dialogue about the rhythm of your treatment. If you're overly inconsistent about going, you may get inconsistent results. Sure, there may come a time when you can go on an as-needed basis. But typically, clients are well served by showing up regularly for a period of time before tapering to the periodic tune-up.

Because the relationship with your therapist is uniquely intimate, it can feel unnatural that one of the first things you may do is exchange money. But no matter how much you come to like your therapist, payment is a good reminder that you are there to receive professional care, not to make small talk. This isn't a friendship, it's a service—and one that should be well worth the price. If it feels awkward to pay, that's okay. It might be beneficial to talk about that in session. How does money affect this relationship? Others? Any feelings are fair game in therapy. The way you relate with your therapist can illuminate dynamics in play with other people in your life as well. In fact, money is one of the hardest subjects for people to talk about, and the therapeutic setting offers a safe place to do so.

If there is awkwardness about your therapist's fee, your ability to pay it, or anything related to billing, it's best to clear the air and reconcile it as soon as possible. Money can be an awkward topic for anyone to discuss, you and your therapist included. However, as with any professional service rendered, your payment is a required part of the agreement. If there is a financial question, concern or change, could your therapist be the one to bring it up? Yes. And you may decide to do so at any point as well. Communication is essential to good therapy, and this applies to the business transaction itself as well. Some of the biggest therapeutic gains come from facing that which you'd rather not. Going into difficult topics, honoring all feelings and processing them is a cornerstone of therapy.

Apart from these preliminary items, you ought to be free to begin sharing about yourself, your relationships, your life, your problems, your gains and your goals. You might find that it gets easier and easier to talk about yourself as you establish more and more trust with your therapist. Before you know it, you won't give much thought to how it works—you'll know the drill. We'll soon focus on just what kind of exchange goes on during a session in more detail. This is where the essence of therapy comes into play.

The flow of your session ought to be easy. At its most basic, think of it as a *"Hello/ Heal/ Goodbye"* sandwich. What varies greatly isn't so much the flow of a given session, but the flow of your overall treatment across time. Length, frequency and duration of therapy depend on many factors. It's pretty typical to begin therapy for 50-minute sessions on a weekly basis. But sometimes it's not that simple. Sometimes people need more than one session per week. If you're working on something and it's especially intense, you might want to go twice a week for a while, or according to what's needed.

Don't be surprised if time flies and it's up before you know it. As mentioned, the typical "hour" is really 50 minutes, to allow clinicians time to transition from one client to the next, record notes and use the restroom, etc. If you would prefer longer sessions, therapists are often flexible and frequently offer 90 minute sessions, so feel free to ask. Your therapist will let you know when you are out of time. It's courteous to respect that when time is up, it's time to go. A quick wrap-up may be okay, but if you start a new train of thought on your way out the door, don't be surprised if you get interrupted with a reminder that "Time's up." It's best to get whatever closure you need before the end of the session, or to be prepared to pick it up at the next session. In fact, "...To be continued" is implied. While you are expected to leave when your time is up, you don't have to tie it up with a bow.

If you've had an unfinished thought, a breakthrough or an insight, you may want to quickly make a note of it for next time. You may have an afterthought, like, "Wow, for the first time I can see how I've been repeating that old pattern. I don't have to do that anymore!" If an epiphany happens before you leave, it's also normal (but not necessary) to take a moment to express gratitude for your therapist, if you're moved to do so. Your exit may vary, from session to session, depending on how it goes and what feels comfortable to you. Some people find it hard to leave, because it's so nourishing to be in the presence of someone so supportive and to feel really seen. If that's the case for you, share about that, within your available time. For the majority of clients, leaving a session is as easy as saying goodbye, knowing they'll be back soon for more.

Because you allow your therapist to know you as well or even better than anyone else, you may feel a surge of warmth towards them upon parting at times. It's fine to express your appreciation with words, but physical contact is not considered appropriate. Depending on your psychotherapist and the ethical and legal guidelines of the state where they practice, touch may be avoided altogether. What's wrong with a handshake or a high five? Maybe nothing. But what about a hug? Remember, as intimate as it is, this is a professional relationship formed for your psychological and overall well-being. We'll get into why physical contact is not part of therapy in the chapter, *What Won't Happen in A Session*. Just know that a friendly, touch-free goodbye is perfectly appropriate. So is a quick exit. As mentioned, it's not your job to be the time keeper, so you don't have to apologize for running out of time. You just have to leave reasonably promptly. If you want to pace yourself to make sure you get closure (at least until the next session) before your time runs out, you can keep an eye on the time, as your therapist does too.

Your First Session

Neither you, nor even the most seasoned therapist, can predict exactly how a first session will go. Just like any interaction with a person you don't know yet, it is inherently unpredictable. The dynamic combination of you and the therapist you've selected will create a unique exchange. What can you count on? Most likely: you sit, you talk, you share, you ask, you answer, you think, you feel, you reveal, you learn, you pay, you leave. You might laugh and/or cry, too. You'll also be getting a sense of the therapist in front of you, as they begin to get to know you with a trained and informed perspective.

Setting the Stage

The first session differs from those to follow in that, as has been covered, there may be preliminary paperwork to complete or discuss. Commonly called an *Intake Session*, this initial session is where you lay the foundation for all the sessions to follow. The overview is important, even if it is handled in written form or covered quite quickly, before you focus deeply on the specific concern(s) that brought you in.

You will have more of your back story to tell, as your therapist first gets to know you. They may ask whether you've had therapy before and if so, how it went. If you have had therapy before, your therapist may want to know what worked and what didn't, so they can serve you best and you can both learn from your past experience. Your feelings about a therapist you've had in the past are important. You're bound to compare a new therapist to the one you've known, and working through your feelings about this is important. Some clients are disappointed at having to start over, missing their former therapist. Others may have had a bad experience they want to avoid repeating. In any case, what you choose to share about past therapy will inform the therapy you're beginning anew.

Other common questions include: What brings you to therapy? Why now? What relevant history is worth sharing? What is your family life like? Social life? Do you work or attend school? If so, how is that going? Are you currently taking medications? And so on.

Is It a Good Fit?

In this first session, both you and your therapist are confirming that working together will be a good fit. Although it's common to get the right therapist on the first try, it's good to know that there are some things that can thwart a good fit on either end. For a therapist, it could be that they're not competent in a client's particular area of concern. They have an ethical duty to tell you if that's the case, so you can find a professional with the expertise you need.

Another rare but possible scenario is that a therapist may feel too close to an experience of a client's to be able to address it with the necessary objectivity. For example, if a therapist's mother just died and they're actively grieving, they may not want to take on a new client who intends to process a parent's death, until they do some healing of their own. When a therapist's life may impact the quality of care in a given case, therapists often seek consultation from another professional or colleague. (In such cases, client confidentiality is maintained, as we'll cover in Chapter Seven.) They may also seek therapy themselves. But if for any reason they feel that your care would be compromised, they must take steps to address that or refer you to someone else. This is just one example. There may be other reasons why a therapist doesn't feel well suited to treat someone. When that is the case, it's in the client's best interest to get some referrals and go elsewhere. By the same token, clients have lots of good reasons for not sticking with a given therapist past the first session, as will be touched upon throughout this book.

Regardless of what you decide about continuing together, don't expect to be completely at ease in your first encounter with therapy or with a new therapist. Although there's nothing to fear, the unknown tends to make folks a tad nervous. If you need some time to warm up and build trust, that's absolutely normal.

If you're feeling some butterflies in your stomach, say so. Why not? The beauty of therapy is that you can be totally transparent and process your feelings as they arise in the moment. Don't worry, you don't have to bare your soul right out of the gate. You still get to decide when, what and how to say what you need to say. Yes, that is what you are there to do. Remember, the timing is up to you. So relax. Ease into it, or go pedal to the metal. This is for you.

Some therapists are dead serious and some love the use of humor. Most have a full repertoire of appropriate states. However, the default disposition of a therapist runs the gamut, as happens with all human beings. Getting a feel for whether it's a good match happens naturally, so you can focus on what you have to say and ask, and trust your gut on whether you can work with this person regularly. Although it has been said already, it may bear repeating; this is not a social relationship. It is a healing alliance. It is quite possible that you cannot imagine hanging out with your therapist outside the office. That's cool, because you will not be hanging out with them. You may have a sense that you could otherwise be friends, or you may find that idea completely implausible. That is not an indication of whether this is your right therapist. The usual things that you might get hung up on about a new person may not matter in this context. In fact, if your therapist is a bit odd or different from your chosen peers, that can work well. It will serve to remind you, as things get very personal for you, that this union is strictly professional, even as it is warm, psychologically intimate and potentially profound. If, on the other hand, you find yourself drawn to your therapist in other ways right off the bat, you might want to consider or even discuss any potential impediments to the partnership. Here's an example to illustrate some of the points we've covered:

A 32-year-old woman, Emily, tried out a new therapist upon moving to a small coastal town in California. She found the therapist was nice, engaged and professional, yet she did not return for a second session for several reasons. He stood up across a strangely large, cavernous room from his clients, while they sat down. Standing is not unheard of for a therapist, but it's far from typical. Sometimes a case of back pain or some other reason would make sense, but he offered Emily no explanation. His far-away stance put him in a sort of one-up position, creating an exaggerated power dynamic. Emily felt small, sunken into the cushy old couch in that room, feeling a little like she was on the witness stand, as he paced around the room.

Granted, we go in seeking help from an expert, so there is an unspoken authority figure dynamic inherent in therapy. But feeling like you're with a trained professional is not the same as feeling inferior. Your therapist is a respectful partner on the path, but they are there to serve you.

As it turned out, Emily kind of liked the standing therapist as the session went on, so she might have overlooked his posing and pacing, had it not been for the other deterrents. She found him to be warm, smiling, charming and attractive—in fact someone she could imagine herself knowing socially. What's wrong with that, you might wonder? She was afraid she might try too hard to please him with the right responses, rather than be transparent. If she was too self-conscious, she wondered, could she be real? To her credit, she knew herself well enough to recognize her urge to win him over. She was starting therapy to unmask herself, and with him she felt herself wearing one.

It's normal to want to please your therapist, especially if you're a people pleaser by nature. But you do want to be able to be vulnerable and expose your secret flaws. A therapist is there to help you through the good, the bad and the ugly. So, if you think you couldn't totally be yourself for any reason, then you might want to think twice about embarking on treatment with a particular clinician. If you sense a desire to perform from the start, think through whether that would impede your process.

The third strike against the standing therapist was that he lived in the same small town where Emily lived. Convenient, yes. But too close for comfort. She said it would've been okay to bump into him occasionally at The Farmer's Market on a random Saturday in mixed company. But entering into therapy with someone she was likely to run into often in that small community made her feel uncomfortable. Emily called him up and kindly explained that due to their proximity, she would look elsewhere for a therapist.

If you see a therapist where you work, live, and hang out, it's a good idea to discuss how you would handle bumping into each other, up front. In most cases, it's rare, and when it happens, every effort is made to protect your privacy. Most clients say it's no big deal, although many state that they appreciate knowing they will not be awkwardly addressed in public. You may not wish to turn to your friend over sushi during a surprise encounter and say, "Diane, meet my therapist. She's treating me for social anxiety and low self-esteem." Therapists don't want to put you in a position of having to explain to someone else who they are, nor cover it up when you don't want it known. If you see your therapist out and about and they don't start up a chat, it's for your protection. One of the benefits of therapy is that this relationship is special and we don't have to engage as we would with everyone else. Confidentiality is paramount, period. That said, if you initiate friendly small talk or just say, "Hi," that's your choice.

If you discover that you have affiliations in common with your therapist, such as the same choir or softball league, this could create what's called a dual relationship. When a therapist has a personal relationship with someone, it's not ethical to also treat them as a client. If your therapist happens to be the mother of your first boyfriend or girlfriend, for example, that would be considered a dual relationship. You could embark on therapy without realizing that your social circle overlaps with your therapist's somehow. It happens. Discuss it with them and be honest with yourself about what's comfortable and appropriate, or not. You might want to look elsewhere, to preserve the sanctity of your therapeutic alliance. Remember, this relationship is sacred. It's all about you and you are encouraged to be 100% yourself, confidentiality guaranteed. So, think of your therapist differently than you would, say, your dentist.

During your first meeting, you'll be getting a feel for whether this therapist is right for you. If you aren't sure at the time of your session, take some time to think about it. Be prepared to tolerate some ambivalence. You may want to go for another session before deciding whether to continue long term. If for any reason you know this therapist is not for you, then you are not obliged to return for more. It is okay to take some time to digest your feelings about it and get back to them about further scheduling. If it works for you, and you want to schedule regular sessions, go for it. When it feels right, you might as well jump right in. Beginner's luck is pretty common, as therapists have a way of attracting the clients they are best qualified to serve. Once you have chosen a therapist you like and trust, this extra layer of evaluation goes away and you are free to focus on the work.

Scheduling

Of course, sometimes clients can't make it in for a session or two. People travel. They get sick. They have jobs. They have kids. Life happens. Sometimes clients wish or need to have a session by phone or video, rather than show up. Sometimes they're forced to take a longer break for health, distance or financial reasons. But ideally, your default will be a regular appointment time with an understood rhythm of frequency. This simplifies things for both you and your therapist, saving time for what really matters. It allows you to go on autopilot for a while and not spend precious time coordinating schedules. If you're not able to commit to regular sessions, think about what you're prepared to sign up for, at least in the short-term. If you could go regularly but aren't inclined to do so, question why not.

Let's say you found a therapist that seems like a fit in a convenient place at a doable time for the right price. Yet, you still feel iffy about signing up for regular treatment. Investigate: what are the obstacles? Are they external or internal? Actual or excuses? Reluctance to therapy is natural and understandable. Therapy calls you to do something uncomfortable—change. Human nature tricks us into wanting things to be the same, even when what's familiar is what's wrong. Change can feel risky, even when things are unhealthy, because we fear stepping out of our comfort zone, no matter how uncomfortable it is. For example, a partner might prefer to stay in an abusive relationship rather than find out what it's like to be on one's own. Or a workaholic might resist seeking treatment because workaholism produced wealth, though not happiness. If you find yourself choosing not to go to therapy, ask yourself what's behind the surface reasons. If you uncover a reluctance to do the hard work of taking an honest look at yourself, decide whether it's high time you did so, or truly not the right time. Keep in mind that if it isn't more than inevitable beginner's discomfort, then there may never be a better time to start than now.

It's tough to be a beginner, but the learning curve with therapy isn't steep. If it continues to feel scary after your first session or two, tell your therapist how you're feeling and see what might be done to make you feel at ease. Consider going consistently for a while, to see if there's a cumulative difference. Like physical fitness, results aren't instant, but working out gets easier as you continue to "Just do it." Assuming you're invested in and ready for therapy, you'll find a routine that works.

It's not uncommon for someone to do weekly therapy for a block of time—say 6 months or a year—and taper off over time, to once every two weeks or once a month, for example. Eventually, a client may go to therapy only as needed or discontinue altogether. Therapists refer to this ending as *termination*. There is no expectation that you will continue therapy ongoing forever. What has a beginning has an end. That is normal. It's also perfectly fine stop after a period of time and restart if and when you feel you need it again. Communicate your needs and decide together what makes sense. If you feel done and your therapist disagrees, the fact is, you're in charge. Maybe they have good reasons for wanting you to continue. If you're stopping early because you're afraid of change, for example, perhaps reconsider the timing of your termination. Think through your reasons and ask yourself why you want to stop. Is it because sticking with therapy will mean moving farther out of your comfort zone? Or do you truly feel done? However, if you get the sense that a therapist wants to keep you coming to contribute to their own stream of income, that's unethical. Don't stick around for them. Therapy is for you.

The course of your treatment will depend on many factors. It's not always easy to predict how long you'll stay in therapy. Many people begin with an open mind and see how it goes. Others have a finite amount of time in mind. For example, a couple may ask to schedule 12 sessions of 90 minutes, because that's what they have allotted for in the budget and longer sessions work best. Other folks set a goal and stop therapy when they have achieved the results they're after. Still others continue with therapy and work on new things. It can feel comforting to keep the door open, knowing that you can always return if/when the going gets rough. Some treatment has an obvious finish—for example if a phobia is resolved—while personal growth work can be ongoing throughout a lifetime. You're collaborating with your therapist on the best plan for treatment, so keep an open dialogue about how it's going and your feelings about continuing or discontinuing, as the case may be.

When a course of treatment ends, it's best to allow some time for closure. How much time? That may depend on how long you've seen your therapist and the reason for the conclusion. You could begin to talk about it as soon as you like. You might begin to address it several months in advance of your leave, or a few weeks ahead, or even just during your final session—depending on the case. Even if it's uncomfortable, it's a good idea to inform your therapist of your intention to wrap up, rather than bolt and disappear. Therapy is an intimate relationship where over-communication is better than under-communication. Being open with feelings and seeking resolution is good practice. Most therapists will be supportive and encouraging. They may also be the one to suggest it's time for you to wrap up, if they believe that's for your highest good. Endings may be forever or temporary, but hopefully they aren't sudden or mysterious. Barring any transgression on your therapist's part, it's nice to treat your termination with some care and respect for the process, your therapist, and yourself.

I once saw a young couple who sought therapy to work on

conflict resolution. We worked on helping them to communicate effectively without things escalating into a shouting match. It seemed to be going well.

When they failed to reach out to schedule more sessions, I was left wondering why. Had our work together been helpful? Had they broken up? Had there been an emergency? Granted, clients don't have to explain when they make a decision to leave, but therapists genuinely care about them and their well-being.

A few weeks after their disappearance, I got a voicemail from the male partner in the couple. He thanked me for our time together and the techniques they'd learned. He assured me that therapy had been very helpful to them and highlighted some specific examples of how. He further shared that they had an opportunity to receive couples' counseling at no cost, because of a job change. He wanted me to know that they appreciated the gains made and the work we'd done, and assured me that their choice to continue elsewhere was strictly financial.

Even though he wasn't obliged to explain what had happened, the fact that he took the time to do so made all the difference in how I regarded that case. Would it have been nice to have a session or two together to review their goals and gains, reinforce their progress, share insights and identify areas for further attention? Yes. Yet in this case, the simple phone call of sincere thanks and goodbye was thoughtful, appropriate and deeply appreciated.

Let's Talk About You

With tactical matters out of the way, we come to the essence of therapy. This is your chance to speak freely. You can share about yourself and your life, what you came for and what you hope to get out of your time in therapy. Usually, this begins with some context. Think of it like telling your story. You can just share what's relevant or take your time and provide as much background as you like. There is no rush, so how much you want to inform them is up to you.

Out of respect for you and your time, your therapist may go silent soon after you've said hello and taken your seat. That is perfectly acceptable. Time to get down to business. Quiet as they may be, your therapist will not be passive as you disclose. Even as they listen, they are doing their job; observing, empathizing, validating, gaining insight and gathering data for your treatment plan. As you begin to talk, remember that there is no one right way, and there certainly is no expectation that you are familiar with how therapy works. Don't stress about it. The therapist is trained to make you feel comfortable and safe and to guide you through the process. Once you have a rapport, you will be able to say more easily what's on your mind and in your heart.

After you arrive, you will most likely be invited to sit on a chair or couch across from or near your therapist's chair. You will probably spot the usual tissue box nearby. You can begin talking or asking questions, and your therapist will most likely ask questions as well—not to put you in the hot seat, but just to get to know you. If you need a tissue, grab one. You can cry freely—it happens all the time. Then again, you may never shed a tear in the room. That's fine too. Most likely, you will spot a clock in the room. The therapist may place it so that only they see it (remember, they are the time keeper), or they may have it oriented so both of you can easily glance at it and get a gauge on your time. If you can't see the clock, you can always ask how much time you have remaining.

The therapist will be curious about you. Although you may find them warm and engaging, they will not be disclosing much personal information, if any, in return. Take advantage of the spotlight to the fullest. You can afford to take off the usual social masks and reveal yourself. It may not happen in the first session, but once you establish a comfort level, you ought to be able to speak your truth without hesitation. Your therapist is a confidante of a different color. They will know your deepest secrets and, like Vegas, what happens in the therapy room stays in the therapy room. Spill it.

You might be thinking, "I have a long story—how could I possibly tell it in one session?" Most likely, you won't. Other than specific types of therapy designed to be short term, like brief therapy, this isn't meant to be a quick and dirty fix. It will hopefully be a long-term relationship that, ideally, will go on for a number of months or years. That doesn't mean you have to attend weekly forever. It just means that once a foundation of understanding and objectives is established, you may tap and build upon that as needed. Each session is an investment, because your therapist knows you better over time. The hour(ish)-long sessions are meant to be luxurious—there is no rush. Give as much preliminary background as you feel important. Although there is usually an information dump in the beginning, the process of disclosure and discovery is not linear. For example, a client may give background, then focus on present-day concerns and suddenly unearth something unexpected that they want to address and heal from the past. Ongoing therapy can be more like a zigzag or even circles than a straight line. There isn't a presupposed trajectory, unless you're seeing a very specific kind of therapist who follows a protocol appropriate for a particular diagnosis. If that's the case, you'll know what to expect from the beginning. Even then, there will inevitably be some interesting detours.

Your therapist will probably ask you questions as you share about yourself. They aren't trying to interrupt or throw you off course. They just want to be sure they fully understand what matters and what it all means to you. Think of your therapist as a wise and curious partner in exploration. As you explain things, you might find your own understanding deepening, and more questions or even insights arising without your therapist saying a thing. The kinds of questions they ask may differ from those you're used to. That's good. Your therapist is like a detective, searching for relevant data that will be helpful in creating a game plan. Go with it.

When you're just starting out, explaining who you are and why you came, you can go back as far as you like, or focus on what's more recent. Even young people have lived a lot of life by the time they go to therapy. If you stay more current, your therapist will ask about your past as they see fit. An emphasis on childhood is very common but may vary by therapist. Some people have formative events that are important to disclose. For example, if you suffered a trauma, it may be appropriate to share about that, even if that's not exactly what you're there to address. Your upbringing will be relevant at some point as well, so you may touch upon it in the beginning and come back to it and fill in blanks as things unfold. Some clients recount a list of historical milestones, no matter how easy or hard, just to get as much information out initially as possible. Others will go to therapy for a year or more without mentioning something very intense. They may have already made peace with it, or have more current concerns to focus on, and that's perfectly fine. These things have a way of unearthing organically when it's important. Sometimes a forgotten event resurfaces when triggered or for no apparent reason at all. If old stuff keeps coming up, that's normal. That's good. Connections continue to be made throughout the journey. It can be mysterious, but trust the process.

The Kinds of Things You and Your Therapist Will Talk About

Once you've talked about your background and why you've come, then what? Then the real work begins. Some clients enter the room and know *exactly* what it is they want to address.

Others just have a sense that something is askew and they need help figuring out what that is and what to do about it. Still others are committed to personal growth and keep a therapist as part of their ongoing wellness routine, rain or shine, as life would have it. When things are on the sunny side, there are always things to delve into—like peak performance or self-knowledge. When you find the right fit, you'll see what a game-changer it can be.

Regardless of how well-defined your intentions may be, you'll want to spend some time discussing your expectations together up front. To keep you on track, it's good to have some goals established in the beginning. Defining goals, too, is a process that differs among therapists and clients. You may never specifically use the term "goals." If you go in knowing what you want to focus on and what kind of changes you're looking for, that may be direction enough. On the other hand, some therapists will write down your agreed upon objectives and use those as a guide for each session. Others may even draft a "contract" of sorts. The idea is that you begin with an agreed-upon target, so you have structure, accountability and a way to measure progress. Granted, goals can be revised along the way, as they are achieved or priorities shift. But whether you go in with a problem, an inner exploration or a solution in mind, you are going for a reason. You'll want to clarify that up front. You may want to consider the question, "How will we know when we get there?" The answer, identified by you and your therapist, can light the way.

Beyond your history and goals, there are many things you may discuss with your therapist. Your history has to do with your past. Your goals have to do with your future. But even as those are considered, the good stuff is to be found in the present. What unfolds real time, during your therapy session, is important and revealing. Just by relating with your therapist, you're engaging in a process of learning and self-discovery. What you talk about may be secondary to the dynamic that unfolds moment to moment in the room. Sure, it doesn't hurt to know ahead of time what you wish to address, but it's not like writing an essay or giving a speech. You don't need to have a tidy beginning, middle and end to get value. Therapy is meant to relieve stress, so don't stress about doing it "right." There is no particular right way.

Even when you have an idea what you'd like to talk about, you may hit upon a more important direction as it flows. So don't overthink it. Therapy is meant to be a place where you can speak freely and explore your inner world limitlessly. In general, say what you need to say. If you're wondering if a topic is appropriate, ask your therapist. Chances are, the answer is yes. That said, there may be a case when material is better suited for another type of professional. For example, if a client has chronic pain, therapy may offer support in dealing with that. However, a therapist isn't trained to give medical advice, assuming they aren't also an MD. When what you need goes beyond the scope of therapy, you may be referred to someone better suited to address your needs. We'll touch upon this in the next chapter, *What Will Not Happen in a Session.*

The topics to follow will give you a general sense about what may come up, but it's impossible to capture every possible subject. The following is a smattering of subjects that may be of concern to a relatively healthy client. Treatment, in cases of severe mental illness, is specific to the diagnoses and not covered within the scope of this short book.

If you consider yourself mostly "together," yet in need of some fine-tuning to optimize happiness, therapy may be the perfect avenue. Just as a multi-faceted human being cannot be fully captured in a selfie on Instagram, a finite list of topics cannot begin to capture what's possible to talk about in therapy. There is depth to you. If you're curious to know yourself better, therapy is a great place to take a guided deep dive.

You've probably heard the old cliché question asked from therapist to client, "How does that make you feel?" Feelings are indeed a focus of therapy. In daily life, we don't always stop to honor our feelings and search for an underlying message. There may be times when you're extremely uncomfortable, even as you go through the motions. For example, maybe you care well for your toddler but you're extremely nervous whenever you go out together in public. Even though you can function, there's something in the way of your ability to relax, even when the child is safe. Might there be some hyper-vigilance keeping you from enjoying your outings? A therapist can help you unpack that.

Or perhaps there was a death in your family and you don't feel as sad as you imagine you "should." That's a good thing to share with your therapist, even as it may be hard to admit to others. Grief looks all kinds of different ways and shifts over time. Or perhaps you grin and bear it at the Thanksgiving table with your extended family, even though you worry about it in advance to the point that it makes you sick. Do you have to resign yourself to that torture year after year? Or might there be a solution, once you get to the bottom of your feelings? Could it be that you need some help establishing boundaries, being authentic and advocating for yourself?

Perhaps you've got a career opportunity that makes logical sense but you can't bring yourself to accept it because of strong internal resistance. That would be important to examine, before you make a decision. It can be difficult to know what to do when what you feel is at odds with what you believe to be true. Tough decisions can be good to bring to therapy when clarity is what you seek. Your therapist won't give you the answer, but they will help you uncover it for yourself.

Although feelings often get the spotlight, thoughts are important, too. Thoughts and feelings are related, and one influences the other. If you think a negative thought over and over, you're likely to find yourself in a bad mood, right? Your therapist may help you to notice your "self-talk," and help you to send more compassionate messages to yourself. That kind of intervention can really boost self-esteem—another terrific reason to embark on therapy.

Emotions such as fear, sadness, emptiness or anger, as well as those such as excitement, pride and bliss, are absolutely appropriate to explore with your therapist. Are you experiencing normal ups and downs? Or extremes of mood? Do you find yourself depressed? Is anxiety getting in your way? How are you sleeping? What are you doing to take care of yourself? These are appropriate and typical areas to shine a light on in session.

Sometimes, the highs in life are just as jarring as the lows. Having a healthy child after fertility challenges may be a dream come true, but all that lost sleep and sudden responsibility can be an adjustment. New parents may find that therapy helps them feel better, as they adjust to taking care of others while not neglecting themselves or each other. It's sort of counter-intuitive, but as it turns out, abundance, excitement and success can be stressful. It's like that old saying, "Be careful what you wish for."

More money may be great, but what if you find that it comes with more problems? Financial concerns are a big source of stress and conflict for folks. It's not always easy to talk about money, but you are free to do so without judgment on the therapist's couch. Maybe your book takes off and you're asked to do a keynote speech at a well-attended event, but you're terrified to speak in public. Therapy might veer into the territory of peak performance. It's more common than you might imagine. Even as good fortune graces you, you can find that you need a little help adjusting.

Life transitions, whether we consider them good, bad or otherwise, commonly bring folks into therapy. It could be an event, such as a wedding engagement or a move, or it could be a phase of life transition, like adolescence, going off to college, middle age, retirement or the golden years, that finds you feeling confused or thrown off. Big life choices of any kind can be difficult, and a therapist can help you see things with a 360-degree view. When so called *normal* changes are a challenge, you may want to enlist an ally to assist you.

Sometimes, it's not change that's a problem, but an inability to change. People often seek therapy to help them shake habits that aren't serving them. When a want becomes a need, addiction creeps in, and a person may feel like they're no longer in control. That can be scary, dangerous, and damaging to health, career and personal life. Therapy helps people break old destructive habits and understand the drives behind them. Substance abuse, eating disorders, sex, porn, shopping, gambling and internet addiction are some of the usual suspects. There are many other behaviors, compulsions, obsessions and addictions that can really diminish quality of life. With therapy, you can intervene and put life back into balance. If you have a habit that has become detrimental, talk to a therapist about it. It may be useful to understand the underlying issues behind the behavior. For example, people often use drugs or alcohol to escape unpleasant feelings or self-medicate. Therapy may uncover and help to heal underlying issues and offer adaptive coping strategies. If shame is associated with the behavior, let it be a relief to remember that therapy is a place of non-judgment. Experts who work with such concerns know it's hard to reach out, and they are not in the business of shaming. On the contrary, you can expect them to be approachable, compassionate and supportive.

Perhaps you recognize someone you love in the description above. It's not easy to live with a person who has unhealthy, self-destructive behaviors. Consequences are far-reaching and affect close relations, sometimes to the point of co-dependence. Co-dependence might be a term used to describe a person whose life is shaped around the harmful patterns of someone else. A therapist can help you remember how to take care of yourself, even in the shadow of another's drama. It's difficult, if not impossible, to control someone else's behavior. Yet, you are in charge of your own health and happiness. When you take responsibility for your own life, you help everyone by being a healthier version of yourself, while also setting an example of self-care for others.

This brings us to another common subject in therapy; relationships. Everyone has relationships, and any kind of relationship can present a challenge. Therapy can be very helpful here, because we're often so "close" to those we regularly engage with that it's hard to see things with an objective perspective. For example, it's not uncommon for dysfunctional patterns to repeat with different romantic partners, until a client realizes that they're gravitating towards a familiar dynamic from childhood. Sorting this out can be a life saver.

Apart from examining your love life as an individual, you can also embark on therapy together with a partner. Couples therapy is popular, because conflict is inevitable. How do you resolve it? When do you know whether to stick it out or call it quits? A qualified third party can help. Perhaps you finally meet the soul mate you've always searched for, but you happen to be married to someone else. Primary relationships often last for decades, and a lot can happen in that time. It's not unusual to need a little help when the waters get rough. For couples who also have children, family therapy is also an option. At times, the concerns are specific to the couple. But sometimes strained relations involve the kids. Family therapists are uniquely suited to address interpersonal dynamics in a family system.

Relationship issues can arise at work, in the community or in myriad ways. Some people find that they feel uncomfortable around certain people or groups, which may indicate a measure of social anxiety. When the relationship in question needs to be healed, all concerned parties can embark on therapy together. But sometimes, relationships with others can be healed just by working on oneself. For example, if there was neglect or abuse in your past, you may be able to work through your pain doing individual work. Maybe you want to freely explore your sexual orientation or get support with a less common love style, such as an open marriage or polyamory. Regardless of the specifics, if your concern relates to relationships, it's appropriate to talk about in therapy.

While your history and family of origin are relevant to your treatment, the amount of focus your past is given in therapy may vary. For people who find that what happened before still affects them in a big way today, it can be transformative to "go there." Whether it's something as seemingly minor as birth order, or something as potentially major as an absent parent, if it relates to a concern in your life today, it's worth consideration in session. Psychoanalysis may have given a bad name to the idea of talking about your childhood, because the focus seemed open-ended, never-ending, removed and irrelevant. But when you hear a version of, "Tell me about your childhood," that doesn't mean you have to give a play-by-play, starting from the womb. These days, instant gratification is what we're used to, and most people don't have the time or resources to do therapy multiple times a week, starting with their earliest memories. We want to stick to what relates to the changes we wish to make now. That said, sometimes connecting the dots from past to present will drastically improve your future. The imprint that was created by your primary caregivers and family, surely informs your relationships today. Understanding where a pattern comes from helps to unravel it.

As life unfolds, we encounter an unexpected, injurious or taxing event. Of course, setbacks happen to all of us, but when there is a lasting negative effect, therapy offers a way to work through adverse events of the past to feel even better today. No matter how objectively benign or intense, when what happened back then still affects you adversely today, it's a good topic to address with your therapist. It may be something quite common, like a romantic breakup, or something catastrophic, like a serious accident. Regardless of the wounding, if your feelings haven't been explored and worked through, you may benefit from talking to a trained professional. There are cases of trauma where a person may be triggered into unpleasant feelings by things that remind them of the traumatic event. Something once harmful, but relatively harmless today, could set off a response that is unpleasant or disruptive. Reactivity may be improved or healed with therapies designed to treat trauma and resulting conditions. When a stressor still has an effect on you now, it's worth addressing, no matter the relative intensity of the event, from bee sting to bomb scare.

A middle-aged man named Scott sought therapy because his teenage daughter had been so emotionally abused by her soccer coach that she became depressed, yet she was afraid to report the harassment or quit the team. Although his daughter was already seeing a therapist, Scott found that he had his own feelings to work through. He felt guilty that he could do little to help her and angry that this coach—like one he'd had as a young athlete himself— was, in his words, "a glorified criminal." Individually addressing his own trauma through therapy helped Scott resolve the wounds of the past and sort out his feelings about the current situation. Having done so, he was able to show up for himself and his daughter and take appropriate action.

When Scott decided to confront the coach face-to-face (after witnessing him bully another player on his daughter's team), he felt composed and centered. Scott calmly approached the coach on the field and articulately said what he needed to say, as he'd rehearsed in session. Without therapy, he recounted, he may have unleashed on him and caused a scene, walking away looking like "a total rageaholic," causing even more stress and shame to his family. But because he'd processed his feelings, found healthy outlets for his anger, and learned to practice meditation to stay present, he was able to speak his truth directly, with dignity and precision. He attributes the strides he and his daughter each made to their work in therapy.

Even when life is well in hand, your inner work needn't stop. The adventure of delving into yourself and your essence is an unending and fascinating exploration. What do you have yet to learn about yourself? Have you considered your values lately? How's your character shaping up? What do you observe about your personality? What are your prevailing hopes and passions? What is your unique contribution? How do you envision self-actualization? What's going on with your spirituality? Your nightly dreams? If it seems that you have it all figured out yet there are layers of depth to explore, it might be time for some personal or spiritual growth work. You might like to find a qualified therapist with a repertoire that includes creative expression, spiritual guidance and dream work to help you go a layer deeper within. Many therapists love working with clients who endeavor to know themselves better and feel willing and eager to explore the unconscious or uninvestigated aspects of themselves. If you're thinking that you might not be a good candidate for therapy because nothing is wrong, think again. Some of your best work can be done when you have the freedom to focus on your depths, in a quest for self-knowledge, illumination and fulfillment.

"That's Our Time"

For a profession that's so compassionate, reassuring, supportive and attuned, it might seem quite jarring the first time your therapist takes a glance at the clock and gives you the boot. They'll say something like, "That's our time," which is your cue to exit. It may seem rude, but it's not. It's you both respecting the agreement you made from the start. When 50 minutes, or whatever length of time you agreed upon for your sessions, is up, it's up. Time to go. That's how it works, so don't take it personally. It's not intended to silence you or cut you off. It's simply time. You might have been in the middle of a revelation…but it's time. Part of your success in therapy will be honoring your boundaries, including boundaries around time.

This is important for your therapist because they may have another client waiting to come in at the top of the hour. If your therapist sees five people in a day consecutively, you can see why they would not want to fall behind—it wouldn't be fair to their other clients. You prefer to start on time, right? So does your therapist. Plus, that human therapist of yours needs time to use the facilities, straighten up and shift gears before the next client comes in.

Hearing "That's our time" may come as a surprise the first time. It might be annoying a second time, but you'll soon get the hang of it and anticipate it. One thing that will happen is that you'll learn to go deeper, faster, in order to have more time to address what matters most. You'll learn to shorten the first half where you are "wandering" and debriefing and will get down to the real business of your work together sooner. Before long, you'll get the hang of it and you might just be the one to notice first when your time's up.

4

WHAT WON'T HAPPEN IN A SESSION

N ow that we've got a handle on the kinds of things that happen in a therapy session, let's mention a few things that should *not* happen. Your therapist is practicing within ethical and legal bounds that are in place to protect you, the client. If something feels off to you, it's important to question it. If you ever feel violated or unsafe, you can leave and cease treatment. Psychotherapists are expected to do no harm. They are there to help you heal. Keep that in mind. You should feel safe and supported in the therapy room. You may sometimes be challenged, or you may feel uncomfortable as material surfaces. That goes with the territory of self-inquiry. But you should never feel afraid for your safety or question whether your well-being is top priority.

It would be ideal to assure you that no therapist will do you harm, just as it would be ideal to elect only presidents who never make mistakes, but human beings don't come with ironclad guarantees. You must look out for yourself in this relationship as in all others. While people typically choose healing professions to do good, things can sometimes go wrong. What follows are a few examples of what should not happen in a therapy session.

Outside the Office Friendship

This is tricky territory, because the therapeutic relationship is intimate, important and intense in its own way. It can feel like your therapist knows you better than anyone else in the world. That may be true, but remember, a therapist is not the same as a friend. That's a good thing! Trust this. It may feel very compelling to engage in a social life with your therapist outside the office. You might quite innocently think, you have such a great time during your 50-minute hour, why not go out for coffee sometime? The inclination to engage beyond your usual sessions is extremely common. Sometimes it's unspoken, and sometimes it's discussed in session. Your therapist may also recognize the friendship potential you share, were it not for the roles you've agreed upon. But this relationship is in a category of its own.

The therapeutic alliance is based on *your* highest good. It's not meant to be a reciprocal relationship. You're paying a trained professional to help you navigate your sacred inner landscape better than you could all by yourself. Naturally, it feels absolutely lovely to be in the company of someone who is endlessly intrigued with you and fully invested in your well-being. This focus is real. It's genuine. However, the arrangement is unique. When a therapist is working, they are doing a very specific job, no matter how effortlessly natural it may appear. If you find yourself wishing for more than a therapeutic relationship, it's possible that you've found yourself just the right therapist, with whom you feel a warm, comfortable connection. If it's getting in the way of your treatment, talk it over in session. Beware of a therapist who has sloppy boundaries. This will feel inappropriate or unprofessional. However, if sincere mutual liking develops, you may get more out of the relationship than any friendship you enjoy.

Two-Way Street

If sitting across from a pal who is dependably receptive, endlessly curious about you, empathetic, validating, supportive and even sage, for an hour at a time, sounds too good to be true, that's because a friendship is a two-way street. Outside of therapy, balance and reciprocation are good ingredients for a healthy relationship. However, therapy is different. You have the stage. It's a one-way street. If you offer some insight about yourself, don't expect your therapist to respond in kind. If they prompt, "How was your week," for example, it's not expected that you ask the same. Even if you do, your therapist will probably keep personal disclosure to a minimum. For one thing, you are paying for this time as a customer. If you want the usual exchange, you could start up a conversation with an acquaintance and do the usual trade. (You tell me your problems, I'll tell you mine). Not so in therapy, which is designed to give you relief more dependably than socializing would. (Although, depending on the content, sometimes that's an okay outlet, too).

Healthy boundaries are in place as a crucial part of the therapy process. It's not really appropriate for there to be a give-and-take exchange because the exploration is yours—it's for you. Not only that, but some therapists ascribe to the belief that their clients are better off with a "blank slate," or tabula rasa. The less you know about your therapist, the more freedom your psyche has to project. So, even if it may seem rude in a conventional relationship, when your therapist doesn't disclose personal info, they're not being rude. Far from it, they're looking out for your highest good!

Although self-disclosure from your therapist may be limited, it's important to point out that how much self-disclosure there will be varies from therapist to therapist. One rule of thumb that dictates that is what helps the client most. There are cases where a judicious bit of self-disclosure on the part of a therapist is extremely useful to the client.

Sylvia's world had been rocked by the unexpected and tumultuous divorce she was going through after 18 years of marriage. She felt scared and hopeless, as if her whole world was disintegrating. She recalls one thing that really helped her put it in perspective. After sharing about her unsettled feelings, the therapist confessed that he too had been through a difficult divorce. He shared that at that time, he felt so unsteady that it showed in his handwriting. "My signature was so wobbly, it was barely recognizable for the better part of a year," he told her.

That bit of judicious personal information on the part of her therapist normalized Sylvia's sense that the Earth was shifting beneath her feet. She chuckled and reflected, "I thought—if this man I respect and look up to who seems so together could be that shaken up by a divorce, why wouldn't I be, too?"

Sylvia had no idea prior to this exchange that her therapist had been divorced. Clearly, he'd chosen to offer a rare glimpse into his personal life to provide her with empathy and hope. He didn't go into any detail or take the focus off of Sylvia. What he shared was just enough to make her feel deeply understood.

As you can see, what works in one case doesn't necessarily work in another. Every interaction between therapist and client is unique. It's important to notice what you experience when your therapist chooses to self-disclose. Ask yourself, was it helpful? Did it make you feel better in some way? More trusting, less isolated, more understood? Or conversely, did you feel annoyed, uncomfortable or confused? If you feel inclined, you might want to tell your therapist whether and when their self-disclosure works for you. Chances are, the intention was to help you progress. But whether or not that happened depends on how it's received.

A tech CEO, Mark, who tried many therapists from young adulthood to middle age, claims that the only one that really worked for him was the one who said absolutely nothing about herself—ever. There was zero self-disclosure on his therapist's part, and he believes that's what made the difference—that's what made it finally work. He reported, "I was always trying to figure them out. Once I knew what they were all about, I felt like it was over and we'd gone as far as we could together. But this one female therapist—she just didn't give me anything to go on. So ultimately, I was forced to keep coming back to myself."

Fixing

Fixing is so natural for us that we often aren't aware that we are even doing it. In fact, you've probably done it sometime in the last twenty-four hours. Whenever we are talking to someone we care about, and they mention a problem, it is second-nature for us to go into brainstorming mode to help solve the problem. We have a strong urge within us to "fix" the problem so our friend or loved one will return to a happy and carefree state. Despite good intentions, however, sometimes that kind of help is anything but helpful. Here's a quick example, found in John Mabry's book, *Starting Spiritual Direction* (Apocryphile Press, 2017).

"I was commiserating with a colleague around a student who was acting out in one of my classes.

"Have you had a talk with her about it?" he asked.

"Yes."

"Did you lay out an 'if the shoe was on the other foot' scenario?"

"A what?"

"Sometimes that works. If the other guy can put himself in your shoes and see how annoying the behavior is, sometimes he gets it."

"No…I didn't try that."

"You could try that."

"I suppose so…"

"You want me to talk to her?"

"What? No, I…"

"Because I know her and I think she trusts me. I could talk to her."

My friend was happy, because he was "helping" me with my problem. In point of fact, he wasn't helping at all, but he didn't know that.

Most therapists are keenly aware of their own urge to "fix" and are very careful not to do it. It may seem counter-intuitive that a so-called counselor wouldn't readily dispense advice and attempt to solve problems for you. After all, you are most likely seeking out an expert to gain clarity and instigate improvement in some area(s) of your life. However, it's not a therapist's job to draw conclusions about what's best for you. It's their job to lead you to your own conclusions about that. While in some contexts a therapist may provide direct advice, therapy's primary function is to guide you to your own inner truth.

The process of therapy works in part because the kind of

feedback you normally get from other people isn't what you get in session. In fact, if you think about it, the more input you get from anyone who'll listen, the more confused you become. When you hear lots of different conflicting opinions about how to "fix" it, you're left to reflect on what, if any of that advice rings true. With therapy, you begin with your internal wisdom. It's an inside-out process—so the best advice you get comes from—guess who? You.

If you ask your therapist a direct question, like "What should I do?" there's a good chance their response will be a question. Like, "How would it feel to do A? What about B? Have you considered that there might be another way?" The answers are within. Yet they can be hard to unearth. It's your therapist's job to help you find them. Can your therapist provide a well-reasoned point of view or reality check if you really need one? Sure. Just know that you might have to ask. It's always okay to be honest about what you want or need.

Although fixing may seem like a short-cut to a happy resolution, it's an inherently problematic proposition, because it presumes that you're broken. Most therapists won't take a superior attitude and presume to preach their own "right" way. Rather, there is trust in your ability to get in touch with your highest truth and make observations and decisions from that place. Therapists cultivate inner strength and self-sufficiency, not dependence. It's good to know, however, that there are some instances when a therapist may be quite directive. For example, if you're seeking help to overcome a behavior, or if you present a danger to yourself or others, they may decide or be obliged to make recommendations or take actions for your well-being and safety. These exceptions are typically covered in your therapist's consent form, so do read it before you sign, so you're fully informed. When in doubt, ask.

Shaming

It's not surprising that some people have trepidation as they embark upon therapy, afraid they're going to be judged by their therapist. They imagine that their therapist has this being-human stuff nailed and, based on that idealized notion, is saintly. But this is nonsense. Your therapist has good days, bad days, challenges, strengths, and embarrassing coffee spills, just like you do. Your therapist may know more about psychology, but that does not mean they are perfect. You may view them as an authority figure, but does that help you open up? Or does that make you feel intimidated and become more guarded? Which way of viewing your therapist will help you get the most out of it —as a peer on the path or an intimidating superior? Chances are, you will do better if you can feel comfortable, be vulnerable, and keep it real. Your therapist may be an expert on matters relevant to your counseling goals, but ultimately, no one is more of an authority on you than you. Don't let an imagined power dynamic stand in your way. A good therapist is not on a power trip. They regard you as an equal, with much respect.

Yes, you are seeing a trained professional because they know a thing or two. You deserve to trust your therapy to someone trained, licensed and experienced. But it's not their job to pass judgement on you. You may be afraid that if you reveal your deep dark secrets, the therapist will make you feel worse about yourself than you already do. On the contrary, therapists are in the business of healing shame, not shaming. You will not be judged or condemned or shamed. Instead, you'll more likely be met with empathy, compassion and understanding. It can be hard sometimes to be honest even with ourselves, much less other people. That is precisely what makes a therapist priceless. Because they can hear your truth, hold it sacred, honor you and your humanity, and help you heal. Being able to share what makes you feel ashamed, in a safe container of nonjudgment with a trusted other, is healing in and of itself. Your secrets are safe with them, and your relationship and treatment work best if you are totally, nakedly honest.

Working through shame, or a feeling that something is wrong with you, can be some of the most important work you do in therapy. In fact, that might be what brings you in. Shame is a common human experience and therapy is an appropriate way to address and release it. While shame itself may be something you wish to work on, if you feel your therapist is shaming you, it's best to talk about that. Sometimes a reaction can be misinterpreted. A look of shock, for example, may be erroneously received as disapproval. Especially for folks who are habitually hard on themselves, a negative lens can lead to false assumptions. Take a moment and investigate whether that's true. For example, if your therapist's eyebrow raises when you talk about a wild night in Vegas, maybe he's intrigued, or maybe there's a trace of envy in his expression. When in doubt, clarify. "You raised an eyebrow. Do you disapprove?" The therapist may smile and say, "On the contrary. It sounds like a worthwhile adventure. Please continue..."

At times, your therapist may express concern that could be misinterpreted as disapproval. Understand that your care is their responsibility, and sometimes a word of caution or advice is warranted. If you engage in risky behavior, your therapist is likely to point it out. They aren't telling you what to do, they're looking out for your well-being. A question like, "Did you have safe sex?" isn't meant to be judgey. It's meant to prompt you to advocate for your own health and safety. Be careful how you interpret your therapist's words. Therapists aren't punitive. They're on your side. So if they make a suggestion, they're presumably coming from a place of support, not judgment. But if you do find yourself feeling judged, that's important to investigate together. Instead of making assumptions about what your therapist thinks about you or your actions, bring it up. Ask. Talk about it. You may be pleasantly surprised what you find out.

In the unlikely event that your therapist is unprofessional and causes harm by judging or shaming you, you can simply leave and not go back. Remember that you are in control here. However, you'll most likely find that if you lay out your deepest and darkest secrets, your therapist will get it. They will have compassion and empathy for you and understand your process and your decisions. Therapy is a shame-free zone. That's one of the reasons it totally rocks!

Sex

It should go without saying that sex is never a part of professional psychotherapy. However, it is worth emphasizing, so there is no question or confusion: sex between therapist and client is highly unethical. Your therapist, properly trained and licensed, is fully aware of this. It may seem preposterous to imagine, yet just as a desire for friendship beyond the client-therapist relationship is easy to understand, a desire for physical intimacy could surface as well. While there is a kind of intimacy that occurs in therapy, it remains platonic. Many feelings can come up during the course of treatment and noticing some attraction to your therapist is completely normal. Gratitude, mutual respect, and adoration are typical, with or without any attraction. When there is an attraction, your therapist may explore that with you through discussion. Much can be learned when you feel the freedom to share feelings of all kinds. Often, the sharing of such material leads to growth for the client and a better therapeutic relationship.

Effective psychotherapy is built upon a comfortable connection, so feeling drawn to your therapist is natural. But while an attraction between you and your therapist may be innocent,

acting on it is not. This is not simply a moral issue, it is one of
client safety.

Gabe, a mature married man, had been in therapy with Dr.
Elizabeth Blackwell for 17 months. He'd been able to
speak freely about anything with her, including his
relationship with his wife. Well into his treatment, Gabe
became aware of what he considered "a crush" on Dr.
Blackwell, whom he called Liz. He decided to confess this
to her, rather than keep it a secret. Liz listened kindly as
he shared his recent desire to know her more intimately.
She explained that it's quite normal to experience
affectionate feelings towards one's therapist and invited
him to share about what he imagined, if he felt inclined to
do so. She also reminded him that nothing would actually
happen between them, beyond the professional therapeutic
relationship.

Gabe was relieved that his confession was met with an
invitation to talk about his feelings. He went on to share a
detailed fantasy of running off with Liz to the wine
country, where they would spend a romantic weekend
together. Over the next several sessions, his erotic feelings
were respectfully explored as he continued therapy. Gabe
found that having the space to talk about his desires freely
allowed them to dissipate. He was grateful that he could
be honest and open and learned a lot about himself in the
process. Gabe appreciated the ability to work through his
feelings rather than bury them or bail on therapy. He was a
little embarrassed, given that it was out of his comfort
zone to admit his fleeting infatuation. But he did not feel
shame, as his therapist normalized the experience.

Thoroughly processing his feelings towards his
therapist, to Gabe's surprise, ultimately allowed him to

realize that he was quite content in his relationship with his wife. He was able to continue therapy with Liz for another eleven months until his initial goals were met.

Sexual intimacy in this context is a potentially damaging proposition, and your licensed therapist has a responsibility to do you no harm. If you feel violated in any way—sexually or otherwise—you should terminate the therapy, no explanation required. You may also choose to report the case to your therapist's licensing board or professional organization or local agencies or authorities.

Beyond the Scope

It may seem logical that if your psychotherapist can treat you for mental health, they can give you medical advice or other kinds of guidance. However, that's not a safe assumption. Therapists have a scope of practice, like other healthcare professionals, which limits them to offer the services they're specifically educated, trained, and legally licensed to render. For example, while a psychiatrist (MD) can prescribe medications, a Marriage and Family Therapist (MFT) cannot. Dispensing medication, including psychopharmaceuticals, is beyond the scope of practice for MFTs. So just as you wouldn't go to the shoe repair place to get your pants hemmed, you wouldn't go to an MFT expecting to leave with a bottle of anti-depressants. You'll need a psychiatrist for that. Likewise, if you're after psychological testing, you may be wise to choose a psychologist (PhD or PsyD), who is well suited to administer assessments.

Ask yourself what you're hoping to get out of therapy and choose a professional who is skilled in your area of concern. As you might imagine, guidance outside the bounds of competency is not appropriate. For example, if you really need legal, financial or medical advice, find yourself an expert to match. Yes, therapists can help you work through the emotional intensity or mental stress associated with any kind of problem. Yet, know that they don't go about solving those problems in ways beyond which they are qualified. Sometimes a therapist will be able to offer a referral to another kind of professional, who can better address a specific concern.

5

THINGS THERAPISTS SAY

Therapy sessions are unpredictable. Even when there is some sort of agenda on your part, it's impossible to know exactly how it will unfold. It's hard to know for sure what the session will be like or what wisdom will be revealed. It happens in the doing of it. It's best to keep an open mind and flow with what arises. If you get way off track, you can always correct your course. However, it's your therapist's job to help you with that, so you don't have to be controlling or vigilant. They will intervene if and when appropriate.

Despite the unpredictable nature of therapy sessions, however, there are a few things that therapists often say or do. Let's talk about a few of these, as knowing some of them might give you a clue about what you can expect.

Invitation

One way or another, your therapist will probably invite you to relax, get centered, and start talking. They may suggest that you make yourself comfortable and perhaps take a deep breath. Whether your therapist actually instructs you to do so or not, it's a good idea. When you come into a session straight from being out there in the world, it can take a moment to "land" in the room, get present in the moment and tune in. Some therapists may walk you through this process a few times, until you're used to it. Others may do so verbally every time, and some, not at all. Just remember to begin by tuning into your inner voice, so what comes forth reveals what is deep within you, beyond the surface. After you've had a chance to get centered and focused, you may want to remember the intention you have for this session, or even just that this time is set aside for your highest good. If the session begins with silence, that's actually appropriate. A moment of silence and a deep breath set the stage for the sacred work that comes next.

Once you're comfortable and have enjoyed a moment to catch your breath and remember why you're there, your therapist might offer an opener to get you started: "How was your week? Or, a polite, "Good to see you...", or an unspoken period of quiet in the room. If your therapist goes silent after greeting you with just a "Hello," that's an indication that you have their attention and you can begin sharing as you wish. They might offer a gesture or a few words that convey, "Please begin." Regardless of the particulars, it's common for the client to do most of the talking as the session begins. This is an opportunity for you to check in about anything important that's transpired since your last session, any insights or observations you wish to share, or introduce the topic you'd like to explore. Chances are, your therapist won't say much in the beginning of your session, unless you start it with a question of your own. Like, "I feel like it might be important to spend some more time on that trauma I told you about. It's old stuff, but it still bothers me sometimes. What do you think?" But generally speaking, unless there are housekeeping matters to deal with up front, your therapist will probably invite you to tell it like it is, however you like. Don't stress about being center stage right away; there is no wrong or right way to begin and it will differ from week to week. Some clients warm up by talking about inconsequential stuff, like giving a blow-by-blow of their day or week. While that's not getting to the meat of therapy—unless it relates to a behavior change or is otherwise relevant—it's okay. It happens. If going deep isn't your style, you'll likely get some guidance from your therapist to get out of the weeds and onto more important things.

Investigation

When you begin talking about yourself, you will be met with a captive audience. Your therapist is truly curious about you and your life. You might even imagine your therapist as a detective of sorts, delving into a most fascinating and compelling subject: you! Just as a detective might ask questions to solve a mystery, your therapist may ask questions to understand you more deeply. This also gives you an opportunity to understand yourself better. Can you expect some of those typical, cliché, therapist-client questions to arise? Yes. From time to time, you'll most likely get a version of, "So how does that make you feel?" This kind of question is not scripted. It is a genuine attempt to get you to do some self-reflection, beyond what you might have done up until this point. "How do you feel about that?" can be a rich source of information, not just for your therapist, but for you as well.

There are many other questions your therapist might ask you, specific to any given session. For example, they might probe, "How old were you when that happened?" Or "What is it about your friend that inspires you so much?" Trust that well-chosen questions are being asked for a reason. This is not the world of chit-chat. If you're prompted to elaborate or delve, this comes with a purpose. When you hear, "Could you tell me more about that?" trust that it's not to keep you talking to fill the time.

Your therapist wants to know more than just the facts. They really do want to know how you felt at the time, as well as how you feel now. They're searching for meaning, and that tends to be revealed with careful observation. It may not be immediately obvious why they're asking, or how it can help, but that's okay. Trust the process and trust your therapist. There's nothing in your answer that can really hurt you, but it can certainly help. Elaborating may allow you to go a layer deeper, or see things from a new perspective.

Questioning is central to therapy; questions about you from your therapist and those that bubble up from your own wise self. Endless curiosity drives us to "Know thyself," as Socrates advised. Your therapist really wonders about you…in a good way. (And yes, they really wonder about themselves, too. Therapists who "walk the talk," do ongoing self-examination, as well.) So, expect some intrigued, probing questions, such as: "Would you share what that's like for you?" In therapy, questions are queen.

Reflection

In addition to questions, it's also common for a therapist to reflect back what they heard, to ensure that they have it right and understand you well. Most of us aren't used to being received by an active listener. The listening skills of a therapist may well feel impeccable, compared to what you're used to. Casual conversation, or the usual exchange at home, may be a quickly paced give-and-take, where one is often focused less on understanding and more on being understood. When you think about it, both are important. When there is more of a focus on talking and being heard, there is an imbalance. Listening is important as well, but it takes a lot of selfless patience—not exactly our strong suit in this day and age of the short attention span. This isn't to shame us for our beloved rapid-fire banter. It's culturally acceptable to jump in mid-sentence to make a burning comment or offer a perspective or opinion, even if that means interrupting. But this half-hearted listening isn't the kind of thing you can expect in therapy. Therapists are presumably hanging on your every word.

Being heard and being understood is healing. Sure, it might be annoying if, every time you said something, it was repeated back and reinforced. But a fair bit of simple reflection is good in therapy. You need to know that what you're doing your best to communicate is being accurately understood by your therapist. Are they picking up what you're putting down? That needs to happen. What we normally get from our casual listening audience is spotty at best. If someone is listening at all, they may seem bored, preoccupied or defensive. Most of us would be hard pressed to parrot back what we just heard, unless we're engaged with genuine and captured interest. When it happens, it's quite lovely. Right? There's an instant connection. Like, "Wow—she really gets me." This perhaps rare but sweet feeling is a must in therapy. Your words and feelings don't get missed. You need the healing effects of being truly seen and heard.

Ready for a bonus? Most likely you won't be just seen and heard, but validated. What does that mean? It's the sense that where you're coming from is absolutely understandable and makes total sense! So, if you shared, "I felt really used and discarded by that lover," your attentive therapist might genuinely say, "Yes, I can understand why you feel used and discarded. I'm guessing that must've been very painful…?" This gets to empathy, which, like deep listening, is another cornerstone of therapy. Not only are you heard and validated, but your therapist feels for you and with you—they can really relate to what it's like to be you. Most therapists have a great deal of empathy, which is presumably what makes the profession appealing to them in the first place. People who can't relate to what it's like to be in someone else's shoes are not well suited to practice psychotherapy. After carefully listening, your therapist can probably appreciate what it must be like for you. When they say so, that ought to feel good, too.

Interpretation

After all that listening, it makes sense that your therapist would have an observation, a theory or an insight to offer at times. Such expertise may be just what you came for. This is not the kind of armchair analysis you get from well-meaning friends. It's an expert assessment, delivered in a way that's unique to you, your therapist, and the kinds of challenges you're working through. When your therapist offers feedback, trust that their commentary is thoughtfully considered. That doesn't mean you'll always agree with them. It just means that they take great care with the content and delivery of their words. Although it should feel natural and comfortable when they interpret for you, this isn't just conversation. They're making an intentional effort to move you towards your goals by shedding light on the situation.

Sometimes, therapists make a guess that you can disagree with or confirm as the case may be. What they offer is most likely a hypothesis, "for your consideration," rather than a declaration. They may connect the dots and check with you to learn whether a conclusion rings true. For example, a therapist might ask something like this: "Is it possible that your difficulty accessing feelings now has to do with the fact that there wasn't much space for you to express them growing up?" If you're asked whether something is true for you, answer with honesty. You could say, "Yes, that's for sure. I was expected to soldier on no matter what. No one ever asked me how I felt." Or, you might correct them, as in, "No, I had outlets for my feelings. That's not it..." and that might prompt your own explanation, e.g., "I think it's because, if I'm honest about how I feel, I'll have to face what needs to change and that could really hurt people." In this way, an erroneous theory leads you to an important epiphany: "Aha...!" And your therapist resonates with the explanation you arrived at on your own. The process of interpretation will be an organic collaboration that drives you to understand yourself and be understood.

In some cases, depending on many factors, you may ask for or receive a diagnosis. Some clients find this very helpful. It can be liberating to know there's a name for that with which you suffer, and you're not alone. *Hey, look at that. It's a thing!* And, since it's "a thing," there are presumably tried and true adaptive ways to address it. *Hallelujah!* Other people are ambivalent or resistant to a diagnosis. *If I qualify for a diagnosis, is there something super wrong with me?* No. It simply means that the latest edition of the DSM (Diagnostic and Statistical Manual), used by mental health professionals, includes a set of criterion that adequately matches what's going on for you. If there is a name for it, it may be easier to find information out there that can help you.

Giving a diagnosis isn't meant to slap a label on you, thereby "pathologizing" you. Your therapist knows that you're an evolving, complicated, dynamic human being and you can't be summed up with a code. However, it can be useful and/or necessary to have a diagnosis, so that a treatment plan can be developed accordingly. Just as there's a wide spectrum of reasons to seek therapy, there's a broad spectrum of diagnoses and varying needs for one. For example, if you expect to use insurance, you'll need to comply with your insurance company's diagnostic requirements. On the other hand, if you're paying out of pocket for some personal growth, relationship fine-tuning or just to have someone to talk to, the topic of diagnosis may never come up. Just know that if you don't receive a diagnosis, that doesn't mean your problem isn't real. Pretty much everyone could benefit from seeing a therapist at some point in a lifetime, with or without a diagnosis.

Treatment

Once the issues at hand are identified and agreed upon, your therapist will help you problem-solve. Try to be open to suggestions. Once you experience the healing effects of a technique, like some of those to follow, you can put it in your toolbox and take it with you. Your therapist may offer many practical coping strategies, as well as helpful information to educate you, during the course of your treatment. You may be invited to do exercises in session, or homework between sessions. Your therapist may suggest some reading for you to do on your own, or offer a short breathing or meditation technique to try. Suggestions like these are typically optional, so it's likely to be served up as an invitation for you to agree to or decline. You may be surprised what works when you keep an open mind and surrender to the process.

You can expect that your therapist will work with you towards your goals with a well-thought-out strategy. Your therapist will formulate a game plan to help you address the thoughts, behaviors, and/or feelings that brought you in. Your therapist is likely to check in with you from time to time, to ask how therapy is going for you and what's working or not working. If you want to talk about whether your treatment is on track, feel free to address that any time. The most important determinant of your treatment is you. You are in charge of your change, as we'll discuss in the next chapter.

Tools Your Therapist Might Use

Therapists are trained in the use of many different tools and techniques; the most common being the tried and true process of listening, reflecting back and asking questions. Although that may seem deceptively simple, there's more going on than meets the eye. Perhaps it bears repeating that this is not a conversation.

It's a sacred exchange, within a safe container, with an expert witness and guide. The healing power of being truly heard, seen and understood within this context is the foundation of therapy.

To enhance this process, there are myriad ways a therapist might work with you. Tools come from a vast range of theoretical orientations, which are too numerous to cover within these pages. Theoretical underpinnings may or may not be of particular interest to clients. If you're intrigued, information is readily available on the internet and you can always ask questions of potential therapists you're considering.

So, how might your therapist's approach inform your therapy? For example, a transpersonal therapist may ask about your spiritual life, an interpersonal therapist may be very curious about your relationships, and a psychodynamic therapist may want to explore how patterns from the past still affect you today. Even within a given framework, however, there is no set formula. Many therapists are eclectic, at least to some degree, and employ the most appropriate approach and tools for a given case or circumstance.

There are many specific tools or interventions that a therapist might employ. Preferences for various tools vary widely among therapists and clients alike. The kinds of tools utilized may depend on the condition being treated, the age of the client, the expertise and style of the therapist, and the appropriateness of a given intervention during treatment.

Here are just a few examples from the many techniques you might come across in therapy. For more information, ask your therapist if there are any specific approaches, tools or techniques they tend to use, or do some research to learn what's out there. There are many creative and even fun ways to facilitate healing with psychotherapy, which you may come across in session or learn about through your own exploration.

CBT. Cognitive behavioral therapy (CBT), is a common type of talk-therapy that has proven effective for many psychological concerns. A typical CBT intervention might involve identifying problematic thought patterns and/or behaviors, and modifying them to help clients feel better. CBT is based on the premise that thoughts and behaviors directly relate to one's psychological and emotional state. Thus, by shifting attitudes and habits towards health, a client may attain their goals. Here's a simple example:

Fred has a habit of putting himself down. He learned to be critical of himself from his father, who pointed out Fred's shortcomings daily when he was growing up. As a result, Fred learned to speak to himself the same way, although he wasn't aware of the habit and the damage it was causing until he started therapy. With the help of his therapist, Phillip, Fred came to realize that he was continually reinforcing negative beliefs about himself. This was contributing to debilitating low self-worth and mild depression.

In this case, Phillip worked with Fred to examine his self-talk closely. Fred became aware that he regularly thought or said things to himself like, "I'm stupid" and "I can't do anything right." With this recognition, Fred was able to notice and stop reinforcing such negative thoughts and beliefs automatically. Eventually, he was able to replace those toxic thoughts with more supportive and positive ones that he believed to be true. As a result, Fred began to feel good about himself and his outlook for the future.

There are many interventions that a CBT therapist might employ. Indeed, various modalities influenced by CBT continue to emerge and gain popularity. These include Acceptance and Commitment Therapy (ACT), Dialectical Behavior Therapy

(DBT) and Mindfulness Based Cognitive Therapy (MBCT), to name a few. Ongoing developments add to the repertoire that your therapist may draw upon to meet your needs.

With exercises in session and homework assignments, a CBT therapist supports a client to build coping strategies they can apply beyond therapy for life.

Cognitive Reframing. One technique that may be utilized during the course of CBT therapy is called a reframe. Sometimes, help may be as simple as hearing a new perspective. If you've been viewing a situation or condition the same way for a long time, your therapist may offer a new point of view. This offers you a new and promising way to think about an issue.

Here's an example of a reframe:

David was frustrated and angry with his boss at work, whom he considered a bully. It was a familiar scenario for this client. A 41-year-old executive, David had experienced challenges with authority figures before. There was a sense that he was powerless under the thumb of a tyrannical superior. The feeling of being a victim frustrated him. He was a self-proclaimed "loser," in the face of formidable, domineering men. When we traced it back in time, David realized he'd had this familiar feeling for as long as he could remember. It turns out, he'd had to contend with domestic abuse growing up. When his father verbally and physically assaulted his mother, David felt too small and weak to stop him. It made sense, then, that he'd long regarded himself as a wimp, compared to the giants that threatened him. How can a child compete with a violent adult? However, in the particular memory David recounted, he actually ended up saving his mother's life! I asked simple questions, to reinforce what David was saying, so he could hear himself and realize that his was a story of real strength and courage:

"Weren't you scared to jump on top of him?" I asked in wonder.

"No, I just did it instinctively. He was strangling her to death. There was no time to think."

"Wow. And you did this at what age?"

"Like, 11," he answered with a break in his voice, realizing for the first time himself how remarkable that was.

As he retold this story, evidence of his bravery was reinforced and magnified. We marveled together at how a child could be so resourceful and triumphant in the face of such danger. To his amazement, David could clearly see himself as a hero rather than a victim for the first time. Relief and appreciation for the bad-ass younger self he now recognized poured forth in the tears on his cheeks. Looking at this incident anew with his strengths highlighted, David could see that, against all odds, he prevailed against the ultimate authority figure in his life. He had succeeded in securing his mother's safety, by confronting his father, interrupting his abuse, and turning him into the authorities. He had actually defeated the power figure. He'd managed to "win" in a no-win situation. Far from a victim, David was now able to resource the part of him that was a hero. This freed him up to interact with authority figures with confidence.

Play Therapy. You can probably imagine that talk therapy alone isn't typically appropriate for children. Younger kids can't be expected to have the inclination, vocabulary, or patience to express themselves in a purely verbal capacity. The broad category of Play Therapy offers many tools, including games, puppets, play dough, musical instruments, drawing/crayons, toys, etc., that may facilitate the healing process. Some techniques are specifically designed for the therapy room, such as board games that might prompt productive conversation. However, a typical game, like Chutes and Ladders, might produce the same result, especially if it's a game the child likes to play. If a person of any age enjoys going to therapy, they are more likely to get something out of it. Implementing play is an effective way to build trust between therapist and client and allows children to open up naturally as they feel at ease.

Sand Play. This tool allows you to choose among a collection of visual symbols and miniature figures to then arrange within the rectangular frame of a small sandbox. Therapists who offer sand play may have shelves of fascinating objects to select from. What captures your attention and how you arrange the landscape you create may hold meaning and serve as a window into your unconscious world. With sand play, you may bypass the rational mind to access new material, expressed visually and creatively. Such an exploration is then reflected on and interpreted by you and your therapist. It may sound bizarre, but it's a good example of how a tool might shed light on your psyche. Soothing sand play offers a different way into what lies beneath the surface for you.

Empty Chair. When the issue is relational, you may benefit from the famous Gestalt exercise known as the Empty Chair Technique. Feelings and thoughts towards another person, or even an aspect of yourself, can be difficult to articulate and communicate. With this tool, a client is free to say what they need to say, to an imagined other. The technique involves an empty chair, placed across from the client, where an imagined recipient sits on the receiving end of their message. You talk to the imagined being in the chair, with your therapist there by your side, as a guide and/or witness. If you could say anything, what would that be? This tool gives you a chance to explore that freely, without consequence. It also brings you into the present moment and out of abstract contemplation. The Empty Chair can be a great way to get clarity about your inner truth and be a safe outlet for that truth, as well.

Parts Work. Folks who feel confused or conflicted may benefit from investigating their various parts, giving voice to each one, facilitated by a skilled therapist. Examining one's distinct parts and even dialoguing between them is illuminated by approaches such as Internal Family Systems (IFS) and Psych-synthesis, which incorporates subpersonalities. You don't have to understand these theoretical approaches to benefit from this tool. Many of us instinctively recognize different sides of ourselves. Is there a part of you that's optimistic and a part that's cynical? Is there a part that wants to read this book right now and a part that wants to put it down and watch Netflix instead? Sure, we all have multiple parts communicating with us simultaneously. We're pretty dynamic creatures, as it turns out. Parts work can be a fascinating way to really understand the voices in your head. Who's in charge? Who's reluctant to share? An experienced therapist can help you know, understand and explore your parts or subpersonalities—which helps you integrate your multi-faceted nature into a harmonious whole.

Art. Art therapy offers creative expression techniques that benefit clients of any age. Often our subconscious is wiser than our conscious mind. It is aware of things that are going on within us and around us, relating to past, present and future, that we are not consciously aware of. Art is a great way to access the wisdom of our unconscious minds and bring it to the surface, to consciousness. Your therapist may ask you to do some artwork (i.e., "Here are some markers...would you like to draw your family?") or you may take the initiative and bring in some art to explore during your session. "Art" is a big category, of course, and your favored form is most likely appropriate to include as you wish: painting, drawing, sculpture, poetry, photography, songwriting, fiction, dance/movement, drama—all of these may lead to revelation and insight. If a creative emphasis turns you on, you might search for an Art Therapist. Even when it's not a specialty, creative expression is likely to be embraced by your therapist.

EMDR. This therapeutic technique is best known for treating trauma, triggers and negative beliefs of all shapes and sizes, although it may be used in other ways as well. EMDR generally utilizes bilateral stimulation to engage both sides of the brain, while memories are activated and reprocessed. At its inception, EMDR involved eye movements, hence the acronym, which stands for eye movement desensitization reprocessing. However, EMDR now encompasses other forms of bilateral stimulation such as touch (i.e. tapping), and sound (i.e. tones heard left and right through headphones). By alternating touch, sound, eye movements, or some combination of these, each side of the brain is engaged while a client may shift from suffering to relief in their own way. This modality typically begins with a problematic belief or symptom and resolves in an organic process led by the client and facilitated by a trained and certified EMDR therapist. Although best known as a trauma treatment, EMDR can also be used in other ways, addressing concerns like addiction, or objectives like peak performance. If you'd like to learn more about EMDR and its applications or find an EMDR certified therapist, the EMDR International Association offers resources at emdria.org.

Focusing. Developed in the 1960s by psychologist Eugene Gendlin, focusing offers a way to bypass the conscious mind and learn from the wisdom of the body. With this method, a therapist may ask a client to scan the body for any sensations or feelings. Once located physically, the sensation or feeling may be focused upon. You might be asked whether a word or image captures the essence of that sensation, and what it needs to feel better. Based on the information that emerges, the body can often tell you something that you would not otherwise realize. Other methods that leverage the wisdom of the body are found in various physical and movement techniques, often referred to as somatic therapy. Because the body and mind are inextricably linked, the body offers many inroads towards psychological health. Here's an example, recounted by John Mabry in *Starting Spiritual Direction*, of how we learn from paying attention to our physical messages:

Most of us have had the experience of the body acting independently of the mind in order to safeguard our health. I went through a period last year where I was working so hard that I hadn't had a day off in nearly four weeks. I was running here and there maniacally, trying to fulfill all of my obligations (and to do them all perfectly, of course). Finally, my body simply had enough of it and came down with a massive cold that had me in bed for a week. It was exactly what I needed, and I have not forgotten the lesson. My body knew what it needed, and when I wouldn't give it what it required, it simply took it —which proves that it is wiser than my mind. This is often the case, and we can use this "wisdom of the body" to get a read on a situation.

Dreamwork. As we covered in Chapter Two, dreams have been a focus of therapy since its beginnings. They offer a unique window into the mysterious unconscious mind. A dream journal may be a great tool to keep and refer to during the course of your therapy. Don't be afraid to reveal your dreams to your therapist, whether you keep a journal or not, because there is no one right way to interpret them. What matters most is what meaning resonates with you. Your therapist can collaborate with you to find what might be informative or helpful, as you curiously consider the content of a given dream.

According to dream expert Jeremy Taylor, author of *The Wisdom of Your Dreams* (TarcherPerigee, 2009), only the dreamer can say what their dream means. But if that meaning is not immediately obvious, a trusted listener might offer what they see in the dream, by saying, "If this were *my* dream, it would mean…" This does something very important—it allows the listener to offer possible meanings for the dream, while granting you, the dreamer, full control over whether to accept that meaning. This creates safe space for you to unpack and explore your dreams. Your therapist may be particularly well-suited to shed light as you share what you remember, by offering the insightful perspective of someone who knows you uniquely well. Dreams can often hold many meanings, even conflicting meanings. This is perfectly normal. It's just part of the richness of this symbolic method of communication between the unconscious and the conscious mind.

Your therapist may be able to provide you with a referral for group dream work, if that's of interest, as well. In a facilitated group setting, you may be able to hear the dreams and interpretations of other individuals, and share yours in a larger forum. It can be fascinating to explore dreams together and share curious musings that may lead to insights or even breakthroughs.

Enneagram. Some therapists may utilize a personality typing tool to help you know and understand yourself and your relationships better. One such tool is the Enneagram, an ancient system which remains remarkably relevant today, consisting of nine predominant personality types. Yes, each one of us is unique, and we cannot be summed up into neat categories. However, it can be illuminating to consider how your default perspective motivates your choices and colors your world. Each type has drives, strengths and pitfalls. What matters to you most? What's your comfort zone? What are your areas for growth? As you delve more deeply into the Enneagram, you'll discover that each type connects meaningfully to other types. For example, in times of stress or times of security, you actually look like other types. And your type has an influence, one way or another, from the type on either side of it. If self-knowledge is what you seek, a spin through the Enneagram can offer a treasure trove of insight.

Therapist Suggestions

If you've ever poured your heart out to a friend, you've probably gotten some unsolicited feedback on what to do to feel better or how to improve a situation. That's less likely to happen automatically with a therapist, if at all. Why? Because therapists are not in the business of giving advice. They're trained to guide you to your own inner truth. Your growth and development may not be helped by another outsider telling you what you "should" do. Therapists are trained to help you be the authority on you.

While a therapist's job is not to tell you what to do, they may on occasion offer a suggestion, when appropriate. It's typical for a therapist to check in before doing so. For example, "Would you like to hear an idea about that?" might be the kind of thing they'd ask. You can permit them to share or say no thank you. Sometimes clients don't want to be coached. They can be quite allergic to anything remotely resembling a "should." When that's the case, it's a good idea to decline and say, "Thanks for offering, but I don't think that's what I need right now."

On the other hand, clients are often eager to hear the suggestions of their therapists, since they typically have an objective perspective and years of experience and expertise. A therapist's suggestion may be offered as something to consider, rather than something they expect you to do. Expectations—yours and theirs—can be openly discussed. If you're worried you won't follow through, say so. Some clients really don't want to commit to trying things. Others love direction. Still others want a measure of accountability to help them make positive changes.

The point is, suggestions are just that. Suggestions. Not mandates. Sometimes it might be a good thing to hear and consider. Therapy is a collaboration. It will help you to be honest about what's helpful and what's not. Even when a suggestion is received, that doesn't mean you must follow through. A therapist may offer a suggestion just to get you to expand your field of possibilities or see things in a new way—not so much for you to take it and run with it. It depends on the situation, of course. If you're there to modify a troubling behavior, you might depend on suggestions that align with your goals. However, if you're there to process feelings, such as grief, for example, you may prefer just to be heard. Be real with yourself and with your therapist. Sometimes you might say, "I like that idea. I'll give it a try." Other times you might reply, "Hmmm, I don't know about that…" And who knows, next week, you might even change your mind. Therapy is an evolving process. Your honesty with yourself and your therapist, when given a suggestion, is healing in and of itself.

I once offered an energetic and intelligent, yet very anxious client a simple breathing exercise that involved a bit of counting. He emphatically declined to learn it. "No—anything with numbers just makes me more anxious," he said, shaking his head emphatically. I can't relax with an exercise that makes me think about math." We shared a resonant chuckle and moved on. "Okay," I agreed. "How about we just take some slow deep breaths?" To that he smiled, nodded and began to breathe deeply on his own. As a therapist, I was not disappointed that he declined my suggestion, but pleased. His honesty benefitted us both greatly. We didn't waste any time on a tool that wasn't right for him. His authentic response helped me to learn more about him. And he learned, too, that it was safe to be real with me. The therapeutic relationship was enriched because he allowed himself to be known.

Homework

At some point during your therapy, you may be invited to do some homework. Don't worry—this is not the stuff of school. You don't write a paper, turn it in for a grade and fail out if you skip it. Homework, in therapy, refers to the opportunity to work on your goal, in some way, between sessions. A lot can be accomplished in an hour a week, but let's face it, most of the time you're not in the therapy office. It can be very motivating to have some things to do, in alignment with your progress, between sessions.

Some therapists are keen on giving homework. Cognitive Behavioral Therapists, as one example, may regularly assign homework to clients as an integral part of therapy. The assignment may be something very simple, yet potentially very valuable. For example, let's say you and your therapist have a goal of less negative self-talk for you, and more compassionate self-talk. How do you build that new habit? Your therapist can make observations and teach techniques in session, but what happens when you're alone with your thoughts? That's where homework may come in very handy. It could be something like, "This week, just notice your thoughts. And if you can, take some notes on what you notice." Then you might report back with your findings and continue to build on your progress, with another piece of homework for next time.

Homework may be warranted for working on changing problematic habits. For example, if you're working on controlling your temper, you may have a dozen sessions with your therapist before they suggest keeping an anger log. Will you remember to do it in the heat of the moment? Even if you log what happens and your level of upset once or twice, you ought to have enough to work with in your next session. Remember, with therapy, you get out what you put in. If you decline a suggestion or a bit of homework, that's perfectly fine. See if you can explain your thinking, so your therapist understands what works for you and what doesn't.

Better to admit that you won't do a piece of homework than to quit therapy because you're ashamed to admit it. There have been many clients who didn't follow through on homework in my experience, and it doesn't make me think any less of them. You're in charge of your pace and your process. Do what works for you and be up front about it. Therapy is for you. Homework is intended to move things along. If it's hindering your process, it's best to say so. You're the customer. Therapists aren't mind readers, although they're usually intuitive enough to know when not to push.

Although some eager clients ask, "What's my homework?" towards the end of each session, some don't want to have any to-do's between sessions. Just know that wherever you fall on the homework spectrum, your therapist has probably had other clients who felt similarly. Discuss how any kind of exercise suggested will help you to reach your goal, if you have any doubt. And never be afraid to say, "I didn't do the homework." It certainly happens. A word of caution: please don't use this as a reason to beat yourself up. You're presumably embarking on therapy to feel good about yourself and your life. The last thing you need is an excuse to feel shame. Although accountability can be motivating, healing happens in a space of nonjudgment. You get an A+ just for showing up. Self-awareness, moment to moment, is perhaps the best therapy assignment of all. But there will be no grades. Promise.

6

WHAT YOUR THERAPIST WILL EXPECT
FROM YOU

I n order for your therapy session to run smoothly, and to get the most done in the small amount of time you have together, your therapist will expect certain things of you. If you've read this far, you may have a pretty good idea of what a client's role entails. In this chapter, we'll talk more about what comes with being a client, since many times, informal "expectations" go unsaid. Since your therapist has probably been doing this a long time and often works with clients who've also been at it for quite a while, they're used to the rules. They may ask you before you even start if you've had therapy before. This gives them a gauge on your experience and comfort level with the process. Fear not, if you're new to therapy, you won't be expected to know the drill. Even though your therapist will put you at ease and educate you about the process as appropriate, whether you're a first-timer or it's been a while, it may be reassuring to read what follows for a refresher or a head's-up.

Go In Ready

Your time is valuable—and so is your therapist's. Yes, it's true, you'll be paying them, but they'll still want to use that time wisely. Just how productive your time is depends in part on how ready you are when you come in for a session. You do not need to prepare, per se. The truth is, you can never be fully prepared for what happens in a session—that often proves to be a surprise —even a gift. It's never something you can predict or plan out 100%, so don't feel like you need to write and rehearse a monologue. Do, however, give thought to what's on your mind and in your heart beforehand, when possible. That might mean taking a quick inventory of what you want to address, or glancing at any notes, list or journal you might keep to pick out one or two items that have the most charge for you.   It might mean taking ten minutes after arriving at the office waiting room or parking lot to sit silently and get clear and centered before you go in. (This requires planning, but it gives you a built-in buffer on days when you're running late or have delays due to traffic, parking, etc.) After some trial and error, you'll have a sense of what works best to ensure that you're ready to go when you get there.

A woman in her late forties, Lisa, was experiencing stress and feeling overwhelmed. At the urging of a colleague and friend, she agreed to seek therapy to regain some balance in her over-scheduled life. A pillar of the community, politician, wife and mother, Lisa found it challenging to commit to weekly therapy, adding one more thing to her long to-do list. Although she wanted to give it a try, she couldn't help feeling that showing up for therapy would be part of the problem. As she described it to her therapist, "I have to make my appointments after work and I can't leave the office before 5:30. So I have to race across town, battle traffic and find a parking place. Meanwhile, it's on my mind that I've got to figure dinner out when I get home. Plus I have a bunch of emails that need to go out tonight. By the time I scramble over here, I really don't want to take the time to sit quietly and breathe deeply, because every minute counts and I don't want to waste my time."

After a handful of sessions, Lisa became more comfortable with the routine. Therapy was working and she found it well worth prioritizing. Eventually, Lisa came to regard therapy as stress-relief, rather than another source of stress. She found herself looking forward to therapy and planned well in advance so she could be in the right head space to "drop into it." Learning how to arrive at her sessions calmly, in addition to the mindfulness skills and coping strategies she'd learned in session, made Lisa's investment in therapy well worth making.

If nothing else, be prepared to be honest. Your time is not well spent if you're reluctant to share what's really true for you. Therapy, like nothing else, offers you a safe space to say what you need to say. Be brave. Speak your truth. If you want to get the most out of it, you have to be willing to share about what's really going on beneath the surface. Your honesty is a must—not just with your therapist, but with yourself. Beyond that, the main expectation and maybe the one that matters most, is that you simply show up. Showing up is sometimes the hardest part of therapy, because it's like a declaration to the universe and yourself that you're ready to face the truth. Just the act of getting yourself there on time, ready to go, is a huge act of courage, hope and faith. So, when you don't have the time or inclination to consider what content you might like to focus on, know that being there in earnest, ready to meet what comes up for you, is huge. A little prep prior is icing on the cake.

Carry the Weight in the Session

Your therapist will be there for you, fully present and invested during your session; engaged, curious and ready to go. But will you? Your commitment determines how well therapy will work for you. The biggest variable that determines whether you'll get the results you want is *you*. Even with a therapist that is quite average, you can supersede your goals if you've made up your mind to be all in. Showing up is huge. But *how* you show up is important, too. Check your attitude before you land on the couch. If you're motivated to make the time count, it will. Don't think for a second that it's your therapist's job to transform you. Real lasting change is up to you.

So how do you embark on your therapy sessions? Try being "all in." Attitude makes a difference, as does intention. The process of therapy is such that progress can happen invisibly, incrementally, or quite abruptly, as happens with the occasional breakthrough. But you do have control over the quality of your time in therapy. You are ultimately in charge of your results. If that seems daunting, fear not. Your therapist will guide you, prompt you, and light the way. Think of them as a companion on the path, holding a torch for you, as you take steps towards peace.

Here are some questions you might ask yourself to get into the right headspace:

- How am I really feeling right now? What emotions am I struggling with?
- What happened this week that might be helpful to share about?

- What would I like to get out of my investment in this session? In therapy overall?
- Am I hoping the session will pass quickly without any effort on my part? Or am I ready to make my minutes count?
- Am I willing to make changes in order to improve my state of mind and/or my life? How motivated am I?
- Can I be open and honest, in service of my growth?
- Am I committed to a process that doesn't always offer instant gratification or magically happen overnight?

A willingness and commitment to "working" on yourself will get you a lot farther a lot faster than the idea that you can get somewhere by coasting. Your therapist is there as a catalyst, but the change is up to you. You and your therapist will know if you're phoning it in or if you're in it to win it. If you don't like how therapy is going, question first whether you're doing your part. Your part is the part that makes all the difference. No therapist is responsible for your life. If you want to improve and get out of it what you came to get out of it, you must carry the weight in the session. You must take responsibility for yourself. No matter how awesome or incompetent your therapist may be, change can only occur when you make it happen. For some people, change is not dependent on having the exact right therapist. When they're really ready to transform, an adequate therapist will do. That's because— once again—change is ultimately up to you. Sometimes a witness, a sounding board or a bit of support is all the help you need. Your therapist expects you to do the heavy lifting because the results you're looking for can't be done for you. They will not take charge of your life, but they can help empower you to do that for yourself.

What happens during your sessions is important, but so is what happens in between those sessions. Hopefully, you'll reflect on what transpired in therapy and practice what you learned outside the office. It's great to be engrossed in therapy during those 50 minutes with your therapist, but can you take it with you? Healing happens by applying what you learn in your daily life. So, you'll want to implement changes outside of your sessions, in order to enact and reinforce the gains you make in them.

Here's an analogy that might be useful: having a therapist is kind of like having a personal trainer. A trainer will push you and work you out hard for the hour you're together at the gym. But they can't be with you throughout the week, serving you protein shakes, counting your steps and monitoring your heart rate. When you meet with your trainer, they can tell if you're prioritizing fitness between visits or if you're doing nothing other than working out when you're together. What you do on your own is apparent based on whether changes occur in your body. Ultimately, your health and fitness is up to you, not your trainer. It's true; you get out what you put in. Your psychotherapy sessions and your mental health are like that. Yes, your personal growth and progress are supported and even catapulted in therapy. But it's you who must go out into the world and use the resistance of life to gain strength. Change comes with practice—new perspectives, new habits, and new ways of being. These are reinforced moment to moment, not just during a 50-minute session once a week. Your therapist may be indispensable in terms of showing you the way to change. But what you do with your new skills is up to you.

Respect the Rules

Most therapists will lay out the rules of the road pretty clearly for you when you begin therapy. A consent form may lay out the basic structure for you—so that's a start. Your therapist will go over things you need to know, such as office policies, rules of engagement and payment guidelines. If for any reason you don't feel fully informed, ask away. The specifics may differ from therapist to therapist and state to state, but regardless of the particulars, your compliance with the professional protocol is expected and appreciated. Sure, stuff happens. If your therapist has a 24- or 48-hour cancellation policy, for example, they may make an allowance (even though they could charge you) if you're unable to attend a session due to an illness or some unforeseeable event, like a flat tire. They will likely charge you, however, if you miss a session because you forgot or double-booked yourself. If this happens, it's not a big deal. Clients typically must pay for cancellations promptly when they miss a session without adequate notice. In general, it's best to alert your therapist as soon as you know you're unable to attend a scheduled session, so they're more likely to be able to use that time for someone else.

Outside-of-the-office contact is another boundary that must be kept. If your therapist tells you they only correspond by email, so be it. You won't want to track down their cell phone number and send a text. On the other hand, therapists and their rules vary. Find out what's okay and respect that. This is a professional relationship and the parameters should be very clearly spelled out. As we've covered many times, the client-therapist relationship is neither a friendship nor a free-for-all. Does your therapist respond to emails between sessions, if you want to share an update or ask a question? They may do so, up to a certain specified point. Or they may correspond only for scheduling and logistics. It's typical to schedule an additional session to address concerns of any depth. Find out what they allow, what they don't, and comply. These kinds of rules aren't in place just to preserve the integrity of the work and to ensure your psychotherapist is properly compensated for their time. They're also in place to protect you from becoming too dependent upon the input of your therapist.

Social media contact is another area of special consideration. If your therapist doesn't accept you as a friend on Facebook or doesn't respond to an invitation on LinkedIn, don't be offended. It's not personal, it's policy. There are a lot of good reasons why therapists may not interact or participate like other professionals do on the internet. Paramount among those reasons is confidentiality. Some therapists don't have a website, let alone a presence on social media. Psychotherapists sometimes like to keep a low profile, to preserve a feeling of neutrality, anonymity and safety for clients. Therapy is a profession that regards privacy and human interaction as sacred. If you're curious about your therapist's boundaries with social media or on any front, check the fine print in your consent form or ask. It's good to have things spelled out clearly, so you don't feel confused, offended, or dismissed. You want to feel seen, heard, and known by your therapist. That happens in session. It's good to be aware, however, that the ways we interact with most people casually these days don't translate to your interactions with therapist. You'll be expected to respect that difference and maintain boundaries put in place for your best interest.

7

WHAT YOU CAN EXPECT FROM YOUR THERAPIST

In order to do good work in therapy, you must feel a measure of safety. For some clients, this comes easily. For others, who may have a history of trauma, it's a gradual process. Either way, qualified and licensed psychotherapists make every effort to make you feel as safe and comfortable as possible. When you see a *licensed* psychotherapist, you can be confident that they are aware of and held to ethical and legal standards of care. You must keep in mind that if you seek counseling from someone who is not held to such professional standards, you're taking a chance. There are many kinds of healers out there who claim to offer some kind of "therapy," but they have very different areas of expertise and codes of conduct (if any). Some self-proclaimed "counselors" may be trying to shortcut the rigorous and time-consuming investment that's required to become a licensed psychotherapist. Others may be highly qualified to offer a specific type of help, while not qualified to also offer psychotherapy. These practitioners generally know and admit to their professional limits, and do not attempt to practice beyond their qualifications. Regardless of their integrity or lack thereof, it's important for you to understand your healer's scope of competence, going in.

You may be wise to employ a life coach for a stint of personal growth work, for example, but don't mistake them for a psychotherapist. A good life coach won't allow their work with you to venture into therapy. Spiritual Directors, too, offer apt and expert guidance when it's time to delve deeply into matters of faith, but they won't cross the line and practice psychotherapy with you. (For an excellent resource on what Spiritual Direction does and does not include, see *Starting Spiritual Direction: A Guide to Getting Ready, Feeling Safe, And Getting the Most Out of Your Sessions,* by John Mabry).

When you see the word *therapist* or *counselor*, look a level deeper. If there are letters after a practitioner's name, look up what they mean. A college or graduate degree, such as MACP (Master of Arts in Counseling Psychology) is not the same thing as a license to practice psychotherapy. Most states require extremely rigorous education, training and examination before a person may be deemed sufficiently credentialed to treat you. False or misleading advertising is not the sign of a trustworthy professional with your best interests in mind, so be sure you're getting the real deal. Would you go to someone with a PhD in English Literature for a vaccination, just because they're technically called a "Doctor?" Ouch. A bona fide therapist may cost more, but they will most likely be well worth it.

Your Therapist Has the Right Stuff

Let's have a look at some of the professional standards that are typically expected of a legitimate psychotherapist. Because different types of licenses and different states have different requirements, what follows is not comprehensive. In the short pages of this book, we'll only cover a few commonly held standards that generally apply across designations and locations. For more specific guidelines, look up professional organizations and licensing boards in your area, which may offer respective codes of ethics or conduct for your reference. If you're ever in doubt about your therapist's professionalism, you can lodge a complaint to their governing board. And of course, you're free to cease your treatment. As a child might say, "They are not the boss of you." Trust your instincts and see a therapist whom you respect and who treats you with care and respect, as well. Regardless of title, psychotherapists are as flawed as human beings in every other profession. In the end, discerning whom to entrust your therapy to is up to you. That said, here's a brief, partial checklist of what you can expect.

In most states, you can expect that your therapist has a Master's Degree or a Doctoral Degree (PsyD or PhD). There are many required courses that must be taken in order for a would-be therapist to earn their degree. The specifics of curriculum will differ with each school, although some mandatory core courses apply across schools. Additional years of training and rigorous examination are commonly required, before a candidate may earn the license necessary to work with clients. In addition to completing comprehensive coursework, training typically includes a supervised internship of practice. In this phase, which may occur partially during school and post-graduation, psychotherapist candidates gain hands-on, practical experience with an expert advisor. These required hours of clinical practice, often upwards of 3,000 hours, are supervised by a licensed psychotherapist, to monitor quality of care. If you have a preli-censed trainee or associate as your therapist, their supervisor may be consulted on your case. If you have any concerns about this, talk about it to your satisfaction. It's a good thing for pre-licensed therapists to get expert input, and this may improve your care. As you may guess, supervisors, too, must guard the confidentiality of their supervisee's clients.

As you can imagine, becoming a psychotherapist takes sacrifice and dedication on the part of a pre-licensed therapist. Many people who would otherwise be interested in a career in psychotherapy are discouraged by the prospect of amassing thousands of hours of service while likely not being well compensated. This is another great reason to be sure that your mental health professional is licensed. There is a level of commitment and dedication—even sweat and sacrifice—that a licensed psychotherapist has demonstrated to be deemed ready to serve the public. These rigorous requirements are in place to protect you, the consumer. Psychotherapy is serious business. After all, would you trust your mental health to just anyone? Once all educational and training requirements are met, a candidate must pass the licensing exams required in their state.

Although the road to licensure is long and arduous for psychotherapists, the requirements don't stop when they're finally licensed. You, the customer, deserve some reassurance that your therapist continues to hone their craft and sharpen their skills, as they stay current with the latest advances in the field. To that end, therapists must receive education ongoing. In many states, they must complete a designated quota of continuing education units within a given timeframe. For example, a state may require that a Marriage and Family Therapist complete a course in Law and Ethics every two years, or as specified by the licensing board. Your therapist is able to choose courses of interest in addition to those mandated, according to their focus and desire or need to learn. Continuing education helps to ensure that your therapist is up on the latest research and in the loop on recent treatment developments. These courses, as well as psychology conventions and professional development seminars, offer therapists a chance to interact with colleagues and like-minded professionals who may inform, inspire, and challenge each other.

If a therapist ever needs a new perspective or professional opinion on a case, they may retain another psychotherapist as a consultant. This is not a casual interaction, however. Therapists who seek consultation typically pay that advisor their usual client fee. In addition, confidentiality is upheld and identifying information about clients is not disclosed. Again, rules differ from state to state, so if you have any questions or concerns about potential consultation, ask your therapist or do some research of your own. Some therapists see a consultant regularly, others as needed, if at all. Some attend consultation groups for periods of time. Typically, consultation indicates that your therapist cares enough to seek assistance in order to do their best work. It's not a sign of weakness, it's a show of commitment to providing the best care. All professionals need experts to turn to when they need a little help. Fortunately, most psychotherapists have consultants to call upon if and when such a need arises.

Some people feel more comfortable seeking out a therapist of a similar background. If you want your therapist to have some experience or identification with a particular community, that could be a plus. You may feel your therapist could empathize and understand your circumstances better based on their age, race, sexual orientation, socio-economic or cultural background, for example. Having a therapist with a totally different background has its advantages, as well. You might gain from a similar perspective to your own, but you may also benefit from a very different perspective as well. Give some thought to whether a therapist's demographic profile will make a difference to your therapy. In many cases, it makes sense to go with the best therapist, regardless of their background. However, if what you want to work on might be impacted by your therapist's context, think through what will work best for you.

Kim attended her second therapy session eagerly, although she felt some butterflies in her stomach. She could hardly wait to delve into what was really going on, now that her new therapist had all the background she needed. Dr. Sumati Shah had been recommended by a friend, and so far, she seemed like a good therapist. A petite woman in her early fifties, Dr. Shah seemed caring, curious and intelligent.

As Kim began to share about the conflict going on at home and her difficulty with her defiant teenage son, she was flooded with emotion. Her eyes teared up as she spoke quickly, in an attempt to get it all out. Dr. Shah leaned in, listening intently. Suddenly, Kim stopped herself.

"Wait. I need to know something," she fired with a glare. Dr. Shah sat up straight, a bit startled.

"Oh?" Dr. Shah responded calmly. "What is that?"

"Are you a parent?"

Dr. Shah answered without hesitation. "Yes, I am. I have two children. A boy, 21, and a girl, 17."

"Okay. Phew," Kim said with a big sigh of relief. "I just wanted to make sure because I don't want a therapist who's not a parent. They wouldn't understand what I'm dealing with." Reassured, Kim picked up where she left off, confiding about her struggle as a mother.

As you can see, determining whether your therapist has the right stuff is up to you. Even when a therapist is fully qualified, you'll want to make sure they're able to meet your unique needs. Regardless of their background, your therapist must be ethical and maintain good boundaries with you. You know that sex is not permitted, but there are some cases where things that seem "normal" are not appropriate. For example, therapists have to be careful about receiving gifts, accepting invitations, or initiating business ties unrelated to therapy. It may be disappointing at times, but these measures are for your protection.

In order to become a psychotherapist, one learns to behave in ways that set them apart. Let's briefly review some of the important differentiating factors we've already covered. It starts with the mandatory curriculum. Clinical psychology students learn not to "fix" people, because ultimately, it's up to clients to take responsibility for themselves. Instead, they learn how to help you help yourself. Would-be therapists also learn not to let their own issues get in the way of their work. Part of that involves addressing those issues with a therapist of their own. Therapy can be a required component of a counseling degree curriculum and it remains an appropriate outlet at any point in one's career, ongoing, as needed. Psychotherapists in training also learn to keep the therapy-client relationship professional, no matter how intimate it might feel when deep truths are disclosed. Clients are vulnerable in the context of the therapeutic alliance, and proper education and supervised experience ensure that your safety and best interests are upheld.

Your Therapist Does the Right Thing

Good therapists conduct themselves with integrity and dignity, while also preserving the dignity of their clients. Legitimate psychotherapists who fail to practice according to ethical and legal standards of care can have their license suspended or revoked. If you're curious what such codes of conduct include specifically, it's best to look online, since information continues to be changed and updated. Search according to your state and the type of license your therapist holds.

We've covered many rules of the road in this book and much of it is common sense. Guarding your privacy and securing confidentiality (except in extreme cases that should be covered when you begin therapy) are cornerstones of therapy. Respect for you is another. Your core values and beliefs may be examined in the course of therapy, but your therapist won't try to coerce you into thinking as they do. If you have a religion that differs from theirs, for example, they won't assert an agenda to convert you to theirs. Nor will your therapist discriminate based on age, socioeconomic status, gender identity, sexual orientation, ethnicity, disability, or favorite flavor of ice cream.

Devoted psychotherapists take their profession seriously, as much as they may enjoy their work. Therapists are expected to respect their clients as well as their colleagues and themselves. As you share the most intimate details of your inner life, it's important to feel assured that your therapist is an honorable person. What that means to individuals may vary, but you can expect that your therapist is reasonably dignified and guards your dignity as well. No one is perfect, regardless of vocation, and therapists are no different. However, if they make a mistake, they ought to acknowledge it and apologize. Human decency and good manners do apply. If you're ever confused about anything, you ought to feel free to ask as much as you like until your clinician makes things crystal clear. There are no dumb questions. Curiosity is part of the process. Therapists don't tend to be the gossip type, because guarding confidentiality is of the utmost importance. It's not a good profession for the indiscrete, and it doesn't tend to attract such. Some therapists even like to maintain a veil of privacy in their private lives, making it easier to be discreet. Others might be active and accessible public figures in their community. Regardless of their personalities and lifestyle, therapists worth their salt have extremely high standards for all clients in their care.

Therapists also keep the focus on you, not themselves, when you're in session. There may be times when some judicious disclosure on the part of your therapist is appropriate and helpful. But it's not the norm. It's your time and, frankly, it's all about you. Therapists also generally receive what you tell them with respect and non-judgment. They come into session with an open mind, ready to make space for what you bring in. Your beliefs, values and opinions are respected. Your therapist won't try to assert their own viewpoint or try to convert you to their way of thinking. If what you express may present a question as to your best interest, they may gently ask you to say more about your perspective, but they won't be coercive. If they offer other ways to look at things, it will be to expand your mind to possibilities, not to persuade. Some therapists are more directive than others, and they may challenge you to a healthy degree, make "what if" suggestions, or give homework. But the only agenda that ought to be in play here is your goals for therapy. If you sense your therapist is trying to persuade you to change your politics or join their pyramid scheme, run—don't walk—right out the door!

Your therapist can't be of much use to you if she isn't taking care of herself. Self-care is a big issue for people in the helping professions, which makes sense. People who have dedicated their lives to improving the lives of others often don't know where to stop, and they can become depleted and burn out. Therapists must care for themselves and meet their own needs in order to be as available and useful to others as possible. Simple things, like making sure there's enough space between clients to clear one's head and use the facilities, make a difference in a therapist's ability to be fully present with you.

Just as they may help their clients find the right balance between work, family, and personal time, therapists must do so themselves. A therapist who doesn't make time for play, reflection, rest, and rejuvenation won't be at the top of their game. Therapists, like their clients, need to learn when to stop to replenish themselves. They must manage their schedules, ensuring they're not overbooked or taking on too many clients in a given day, week or year. Can you imagine your therapist scattered, frazzled, and answering phone calls during your session? That's hardly fair to you. Therapists lead by example. In order to be composed and centered, they must know and respect their limits.

Outside of work hours, they must attend to their physical health and fitness, get ample sleep and take the occasional vacation. An overworked, depleted therapist will not be able to provide the quality of care you deserve. Ideally, therapists model a healthy work-life balance and inspire the same in their clients.

Knowing that your therapist also needs to practice self-care is a good reminder that they are only human. Sometimes, therapists can be put upon a pedestal and seen as a hero or idol of sorts. There's a temptation to view them as miracle workers who can swoop in and fix everything. If you fantasize that your therapist is perfect, be assured that's completely normal. It's easy to project idealized qualities onto your ultimate advisor and confidante. However, the truth is, a therapist should never play God. No matter how wise, compassionate and indispensable your therapist may be, they are your equal, human to human. A therapist is not a savior, not an oracle, not the almighty last word. They are simply qualified professionals doing their job, ideally with the highest standards of excellence.

CONCLUSION

Over the course of this book, I hope you've learned more about therapy; what it is, how it works and how to get the most out of it. Maybe you're pleasantly surprised that therapy is a totally accessible, sensible and seasoned option. If you're open to working on yourself, doing so with a therapist is a great idea. Anyone can benefit from a stint in therapy—from fine tuning to foundational transformation.

The field of psychotherapy offers us a way to do deep inner work without having to go it alone. That qualified "other" can catapult your journey of self-discovery to a level beyond what introspection and self-analysis do alone. We need mirrors. We need a witness. We need validation. We need honest feedback. And sometimes, we need a little help.

You hopefully see that the calling of psychotherapy encompasses a wide range of professionals to assist the full spectrum of people. If you seek out a therapist and they aren't right for you, try someone else until you find a fantastic fit. Don't forget to ask questions, stay curious, be honest and trust the process. If you decide to give therapy a go, congratulations on the decision to make a major investment in yourself. I believe in psychotherapy, just as surely as your psychotherapist believes in you.

SPECIAL OFFER

10 copies of *Starting Therapy* for only $85!

If you are a therapist, and would like to have some paperback copies of *Starting Therapy* on hand to give to your new clients, you can order them in bulk directly from the publisher for a special "professional courtesy" rate of $85 for ten copies, postage included.* This is approximately half off the cover price!

To take advantage of this special price, simply email the publisher at apocryphile@me.com.

*The publisher will pay postage within the US only; non-US orders will have postage factored into their cost.

www.ingramcontent.com/pod-product-compliance
Lightning Source LLC
Chambersburg PA
CBHW031211270326

41931CB00006B/517